# *WITNESSES*

# WITNESSES

## A NOVEL BY

## MARCY MORAN HEIDISH

HOUGHTON MIFFLIN COMPANY
*BOSTON 1980*

Copyright © 1980 by Marcy Moran

Library of Congress Cataloging in Publication Data

Heidish, Marcy Moran.
    Witnesses.

    1. Hutchinson, Anne Marbury, 1591–1643 — Fiction.
I. Title.
PZ4.H4593Wi      [PS3558.E4514]      813'.54      80-10608
ISBN 0-395-29196-8

Printed in the United States of America

V  10 9 8 7 6 5 4 3 2 1

*For Anne Nagel Barrett*
*And for Thomas P. Gavigan*

*Much Madness is divinest Sense —*
*To the discerning Eye*

— EMILY DICKINSON


*. . . no story records the like of a woman since*
*that mentioned in the* Revelation.

— JOHN WINTHROP


*And I will give power unto my two witnesses,*
*and they shall prophesy a thousand two*
*hundred and threescore days, clothed in sack-*
*cloth. These are the two olive trees, and the two*
*candlesticks standing before the God of the*
*earth.*

— REVELATION 11: 3, 4

# ACKNOWLEDGMENTS

*I* wish to thank my editor Anita McClellan, my agent Jacques de Spoelberch, Katherine Benedict, Carole LaMarca Steininger, Jonathan and Susan Yardley, and my friends for their encouragement during the writing of this book.

Special thanks to Karen Lubieniecki for her perceptive contribution to the final draft and to Mary McCay, Ph.D., for her discerning assistance with the final phase of research.

I am grateful as well for the help given by Bernard Bailyn of Harvard University, The Boston Athenaeum, the Boston Registry Department, Len Tucker, Marjorie F. Butheim and Malcolm Freiberg of the Massachusetts Historical Society, Abbott Lowell Cummings of the Society for the Preservation of New England Antiquities, the Library of Congress, the Rhode Island Historical Society, and especially G. B. Warden of the Cambridge Historical Society, and the late Walter Muir Whitehill.

There were many valuable sources for the historical backbone of this novel; too many to name here. I would however acknowledge the most important: The Boston Book of Possessions, Chronicles of First Planters of the Colony of Massachusetts Bay, The Cotten Family Papers, The Hutchinson Family Papers, John Winthrop's Journal (edited by James Kendall Hosmer), The Records of the First Church of Boston,

The Records of the Town of Cambridge, The Winthrop Family Papers, and numerous secondary and tertiary sources pertinent to Puritanism, New England Colonialism, and sixteenth- and seventeenth-century England. Particularly helpful were: *Antinomians in the Colony of Massachusetts Bay*, edited by Charles Francis Adams, and his *Three Episodes of Masssachusetts History; The Founding of New England* by James T. Adams; *History of the Parish and Matters of Alford and Rigsby*, by Reginald Dudding; *History of the Colony and Province* by Thomas Hutchinson, edited by Lawrence Shaw Mayo, and the *Magnalia Christi Americana or the Ecclesiastical History of New England* by Cotton Mather. Works by Carl Bridenbaugh, George Francis Dow, Alice Monse Earle, and Samuel Eliot Morison were also of assistance, as was Lyle Koehler's "The Case of the American Jezebels: Anne Hutchinson and Female Agitation During the years of Antinomian Turmoil 1636–1640," *William and Mary Quarterly*, third series, vol. 31, no. 1 (January 1973). Four biographies of Anne Hutchinson were invaluable: Helen Auger's *An American Jezebel*, Emory Battis' *Saints and Sectaries: Anne Hutchinson and the Antinomian Controversy in the Massachusetts Bay Colony;* Reginald Bolton's *A Woman Misunderstood;* and Winnifred Rugg's *Unafraid: A Life of Anne Hutchinson.*

# *AUTHOR'S NOTE*

*T*his novel is by definition a work of fiction. It is based on historical incidents which occurred between 1634 and 1638 in Boston, in the Massachusetts Bay Colony.

Anne Hutchinson lived in a society whose fundamental religious, political, and social beliefs are largely alien to our modern ones. My purpose in writing this novel was neither to examine the theological implications of Hutchinson's dispute with the Massachusetts Bay clergy nor to develop or expound a new history of her activities; it was instead to explore the personal motivation and dilemma of Anne Hutchinson, and to create a portrait of an individual whose beliefs came into conflict with her world.

It is important to note that nothing written by Anne Hutchinson, or pertaining to her, by her contemporaneous family, her supporters or friends, has survived. It is equally important to emphasize that most of what we know about her was recorded by people who were not sympathetic to her or frankly antipathetic. The accounts of her rendered by the ministers who conducted her ecclesiastical trial, the transcripts of her civil trial, made by John Winthrop and Robert Keaynes, and the accounts of the Antinomian controversy in John Winthrop's Journals and in his *A Short History of the Rise, Reign, and Ruin of the Antinomian Familists, Libertines That Affected the Churches of New England* are of course shaped by the attitudes of their authors. Most of the important primary sources are of this nature.

Much was made of Anne Hutchinson's sixteenth and final pregnancy in her time and in our own. Some historians suggest that she was pregnant during her imprisonment and ecclesiastical trial; others suggest that she did not become pregnant until after her second trial. I have taken the predominant view. Some historians have written that she gave birth to a stillborn and malformed child; contemporaries of Anne Hutchinson's called the birth a "monstrous" one, which was how an abnormal fetus was termed. Modern medical opinion sees the birth as that of a hydatidiform mole, based on the account reported by Dr. John Clarke to the Massachusetts Bay elders and made public by John Cotton and John Winthrop. However, this account was designed to discredit Anne Hutchinson before Boston Church.

A note on the calendar is appropriate. Seventeenth-century English people observed March 25 as the first of the year, with the Old Style Julian calendar. To avoid confusion I used the dates as given in the sources, but labeled as occurring in 1638 all dates falling after January 1.

I have tried in most cases to avoid Elizabethan dialect as it is nearly incomprehensible to the modern reader.

# PART I

---

# *NELL BENEDICT'S NARRATIVE*

## *April, 1638*

### BOSTON

*D*on't believe everything you hear.

There's talk of her still; she's gone but they've not done with her yet, they hiss and scold about *that Jezebel.* She was someone I knew and knew well and it's falsehoods they speak; even with both trials over and her out of their path forever.

I find it difficult to think of her now without thinking of the trials at the same time. A damnable trick of my wits. As if that's all there is, as if she never did anything before them — and I know better.

The trials' edges cut into my mind like splinters of bone.

*Summon her.* The crowded court, benches packed, doorway swarming. Wintry dampness; smell of wet woolens, charred wood. Clanging foot-warmers, smoke from their coals drifting, bluish, toward the rafters. *Stand forward.* Her familiar footfalls, the long firm stride in that strange aisle. *You are called here as one who has troubled the peace.* The magistrates mantled in black, ranged behind their narrow table, Governor Winthrop at its center. *You have seduced honest people from their homes.* White breath hanging at his mouth, at hers. Sound of quills clawing across paper. *You have maintained a meeting that has been condemned.* Her back stiff in-

---

3

side the gray cloak, strands of dark hair wavering at the nape of her neck. *Your course is not to be suffered.* Shadows webbing in the corners; brief flush of late sun, wine-colored, across the floor. *Take away the foundation and the building will fall.* Whispers. Her voice. The gavel's crack. *She is the breeder and nourisher of these distempers amongst us.* A hush; the click of a hairpin, hers, against the floor. *It be the mind of this court that she is a woman unfit for our society.* The clergy's turn, Boston Church: long procession of black gowns, dragging hems, forked Geneva neckbands glossy with starch. *Consider the just hand of God against you.* Thin light from the high windows falling in squares across the shifting gowns, her shoulder, the pastor's cheek. *I do admonish you in the name of Christ Jesus in whose place I stand.* Her face half-turned and motionless, lips tight. *Her opinions cannot be borne.* Outside a rising wind, ice shells crackling off the trees, pelting the wall like stones. *All kindness received from her has had poison mixed with it.* A stir on the ministers' bench. *We are bound to remove her from us.* Silence. The scrape of her stool. A rustle in the pulpit. *In the name of our Lord Jesus Christ I do cast you out and deliver you up to Satan . . .*

Those who knew her well keep silent now or have quit Boston entirely and I too am packing. But first I must make plain my mind, tell what I know to be truth.

A fair amount of what I know wouldn't have mattered to the courts, mind you, would hardly be evidence to sway a bench of magistrates. It could not have interested them to learn, for instance, that Anne Marbury Hutchinson liked to whistle tinkers' tunes, loathed squash and craved custard, dreaded winter, dabbed vanilla behind her ears for scent, and was prone to backache. That is, quite simply, one kind of evidence I am left with after having been her friend.

And to me it matters. It matters as much as the other sundry facts I know which bear directly upon the testimony, accusations, charges. Perhaps it matters more.

---

4

Whatever.
To all I know I shall set my name.


Aside from the marriage registry of my old parish church I have set my name to few things of lasting importance to me: only the midwifery and apothecary licenses I was issued in England. I have them still. They are crumbling where they've been folded, the parchment worn and webbed as my skin; sealed, witnessed, and signed in a young open hand I can scarce believe to be my own: Eleanor Nasmith Benedict + Baptized in Christ + Eleanor Elizabeth Bridget Deborah + (Baptized with a striking lack of humility after two English queens, an Irish saint, and a Hebrew judge. A terrible burden. Since girlhood, I have answered only to Nell.)

I fear there is not very much to tell about myself by way of introduction before going on.

In September I shall be two-and-sixty and daresay I show every ring on the tree although my hair has perversely refused the dignity of turning gray. My joints are stiff most mornings and I seem to be shrinking but I am still in possession of my wits and my teeth, the both of which provide numerous consolations.

We emigrated late in life, my husband and I, nearly eight years ago — summer of '30, that was. For a time I was the only midwife here, and became apothecary as well; but in the main we came because my husband's skills as a master carpenter were sought by the Massachusetts Bay Company. We landed soon after the colony was planted and the town of Boston settled on this scrubby treeless spit of land the Indians called Shawmut.

I should hasten to make clear that we did not come with the celebrated "Winthrop Fleet," as people style it — particularly the Winthrops — those pioneer ships which carried the colony charter and a variety of distinguished passengers. Our ship carried twenty-seven head of swine in the hold and no distinguished passengers at all, though certainly the most notable was a gunsmith called Dutchman with six fingers on each hand.

I was born at an awkward moment in the Lady Chapel of Ely Cathedral in Cambridgeshire, under the reign of Good Queen Bess and, according to a traveling astrologer, the sign of Libra. When I was five an effigy of Mary Queen of Scots was put to the torch on the village green, an image as clear to me as the face of my mother, who died that spring. When I was eleven great bonfires were lit to warn of the coming Spanish Armada, and the churchbells pealed all night long. When I was thirteen a woman was burned at the stake in the marketplace for witchcraft; I saw it before my grandmother jerked me away by the sleeve. That same autumn my father's mill caught fire in the middle of the night and stood with its sails flaring against the dark sky; my father died soon afterward and I was taken in by the Cromwell family, who educated me. My speech has lost some of its country tuning and my mind has gained something in the way of knowledge but I don't fool myself.

My people were plain folk from yeoman stock, not a dram of well-born blood amonst us. My father held book-reading in high suspicion along with lawyers and snakes. My grandmother was a midwife, famed for arts she'd learned only by the watching and the telling of them; she made certain I learned my letters at the dame school partly, I think, so that I could read to her from the new *Gerard's Herbal*. I have it still, Grandam's *Herbal*, and shall soon pack it away with care. It is her legacy to me, along with her craft, her gingery hair, keen eyesight, and an urge to sneeze near shaggy animals.

A generally suspicious nature, my father's legacy, failed me when emigration fever began sweeping the eastern shires, a decade ago, when the Massachusetts Bay Company came seeking more investors and skilled craftsmen, when tracts were passed about the fair new land across the sea *(wood enough to warm all Europe — air of a healing nature — fruitful soil beyond belief )*.

Or rather I could not say my husband nay.

We had little tying us to England, our close kinsfolk gone, our home lately flooded to ruin in the fenlands — and dear God, how young it made Rob again to plan our crossing; how certain he was that we would prosper here. His mind filled with plans. His tools were honed. He carried me across the ship's gangway as if it were a threshold and I a bride — I, at my age, protesting — and he fashioned every beam and peg and joining in this new house with his own hands.

About five months after we settled here, he was crushed beneath a felled tree while on a lumbering chore beyond Boston Neck. I can still feel how my throat tightened when they ran to fetch me.

Forgive me, I seldom speak of this. It still makes me weep.

However.

Pity I want not.

Rob left me clear of debt, and my work as apothecary and midwife has kept me well enough. I still dispense physick to the women and children and anyone afraid of the barber-surgeon, but I was glad to give over most birthings to Jane Hawkins, a younger midwife who came last year, and to Anne Hutchinson, who assisted us both; I am too old to be running about in the night.

And so I have managed.

I have twice known ruin, twice survived.

Perhaps it is my taste of ruin that links me to Anne as well as friendship, although her ruin was not caused by flood or mishap or some other act of God that touches ordinary lives everywhere. However, I should add that many here believe her ruin to have been a direct act of God; a direct strike, as with lightning.

Divine Providence.

Anne vanquished, Zion preserved.

So they say.

---

This land, this Massachusetts Bay Colony, as you may know, has been claimed as the New English Promised Land, the Wilderness Zion, the Bible Commonwealth. The great preacher Thomas Hooker has told us that England will be destroyed shortly; Pastor Wilson and Governor Winthrop share his vision. And here we shall begin anew, here, as Governor Winthrop is fond of quoting, we shall build a city on a hill, led by our Puritan founders and all who have made a new covenant with God. Here, as our ministers are fond of preaching, dwell the new People Israel, the Lord's new chosen ones, the newly manifest saints of God.

Well.

Some of us, that is.

Many came here out of religious conviction, true enough; many of us came, pure and simple, for the privilege of owning land, and a great deal of land; for the chance to prosper in the commerce of pitch, pipestones, pelts; and for the dream, the promise, the clean start. Zion needs carpenters and cordwainers and smiths, else not survive, and many a time the carpenter's clever fingers and the Puritan's pious soul come not attached to the same man. Numerous folk are not covenanted church members, far more than half the town, and I am amongst that lot, amongst those who came here for reasons other than conscience.

I must say it is something odd that I find myself planning to depart here for reasons of conscience; if there's a way to do anything backwards I wager I'd manage to find it.

But no matter.

Here in Boston I am known as the elder midwife or as Goody Benedict. Goodwife, not Mistress, as befits my social station and as makes it easier, I suppose, to tell you about Anne. I've no lofty social rank to protect, no gilded family honor to preserve, no heirs. I wish to speak openly and it happens that I can afford to.

But I would in any case, I believe.

Out of affection for Anne, out of friendship.

---

8

And out of anger.

Mistake me not. It isn't the hardships of pioneering that cause me to be about this packing. It is what happened to Anne Hutchinson here and the good people of this town who somehow allowed it to happen — not all, nay, but many. Those who came to her meetings and blessed what she said. Those who welcomed her into the church and gave her their hands in fellowship. Those who prospered her husband and sent their children to roust about with hers. Those she pulled with in childbed.

They were amongst those who sat silent during the court trial and the church trial. They were amongst those who renounced her while she was waiting in prison between the two. They were amongst those who made no move, no cry, when this bad business finished a fortnight ago. They are amongst those who are not gone and are not packing.

I did not expect anything different from the Governor and the Pastor, nor in the end from most of the ministers and magistrates.

I expected more from our neighbors is what.

I am told I expected far too much and very likely that is true.

And there: a fine one to talk, I am. April is upon us and here I am still. Packing. Dawdling? Lingering.

In some ways, it is not easy to leave. There is much I shall part from with pain, as did Anne.

I like the feel of the sea round about this town, Boston being nearly an island; the Neck linking us to the mainland is often awash in shimmering brine. I like the smell of salt and mist and molasses when the wind comes in over the docks, and the laughter of the shore birds, and the gulls arrowing through the lanes over the gables. From Sentry Hill I have seen the sun shatter like glass on the water and in summer wild strawberries glimmering sharp as embers in the long grass. Pumpkins bob along the ground in autumn, funny and magical to me as when first I beheld them. Ice moans with a strange enchanted sound in the harbor during a thaw. On snowy evenings the air is sometimes purple. A ragged tree bites the sky. In early spring the fog is chunky as cheese, but when it lifts the light is often purer and more piercing than ever it was in England.

I shall try to forget all this soon.

But not yet, not quite yet.

Until I have told something of how it was when Anne was here and how it happened that she is here no longer, I shall need to remember. This task of packing distracts, rebukes me, and there are plans to be laid, but it would ease my heart somewhat to make this accounting.

My view.

Not that of "my betters." Theirs is already known.

A friend's testimony ought to be given.

*T*he day of Anne's arrival in Boston is clear in my mind only because the ship that brought the Hutchinsons also brought me a long-awaited packet of medicinals from London; otherwise the day might have slid into all the others of that warm hazy September of '34.

A Thursday, that was.

Market Day.

I was up on Windmill Hill that morning. I had gone rambling up there with a vague intention to collect certain curative weeds; what I truly meant to do was watch out for a ship. I remember gathering an apronful of goldenrod and glancing over my shoulder at the Bay.

Toward midmorning I spied a three-master, its sails hovering like moth wings against the whitish washed-out sky. By noon, top and foresails dropped, she was nearing Town Cove. I started down the grassy slope and across the open fields, along the ragged fences of Christopher Stanley's pasture, looking down on steep roofs pitched over gray weathered walls or raw yellow clapboard, here and there an open casement glinting in the sunlight; down over dry lanes the color of cornmeal, winding into the broad brown scar of the High Street, and, stepping faster, I caught a flash of green stockings, a yellow apron, and heard voices calling and doors slamming and boots tramping as people began coming into the byways, and, a bit breathless now, down past a workbench with a saw left quivering in a partly cut beam, quick past some night soil cast from a window, off past a garden basket half-filled with greens, down to the angling of the Great Street where a crowd spilled from the marketplace with a deep thrum of voices, louder as it swept me up, took me with it, along past the meeting house and over to Bendall's Dock on Great Cove.

The *Griffin* was in.

There was the expected confusion. There was the great crane swinging down freight, there were the two hundred passengers and the hundred head of cattle, there were the casks and chests and crates and barrels, there were the seamen and ropes snaking through the air and the gulls diving on a sack of spilled grain, there were the lost children, the misplaced furniture, the ballast of bricks, the ripe juicy swearing, jostling, shouting, and there, at last, in a pile of others, was my packet.

The arrival of a ship is always something of an event here. It means tidings from England and letters from kin and fresh supplies and new neighbors and brisk trade.

To me just then it meant new copper tubing for my still.

It meant tincture of poppy, oil of eucalyptus.

It meant camphor.

I hastened uphill along the High Street, anxious to get my small crate home and open, anxious to smell that musty whiff of London which I knew would be hovering under its lid. Some of the commotion had quieted a bit by then, people were going in for noon dinner but as I trudged up the road I noticed a good many were standing in their doorways, gazing in my direction.

Happily I am old enough to have ceased supposing all eyes must be upon me; I glanced over my shoulder, turned round and stopped.

A great canopy bed was coming up the slope behind me,

seemingly on its own. Reaching higher and higher above the dusty rise of ground were four carved posts swaying like masts in a light breeze. They were joined at the upper corners by a wide valance frame bare of curtains and the edges of two or three feather mattresses bellied out beneath. I have seen other beds taken off the ships this way, not dismantled and used as a cart, but I had never seen one so majestic, so richly carved. As the bed cleared the rise four strapping men came into sight, shirtless and sweating as they bore aloft this raft of an heirloom, loaded with casks and chests.

Rising up behind the bed like one of its posts was Anne. Anne, sunburned, nose peeling, her hair coming down every which way and a pair of shears stuck through the laces of her bodice and a length of twine swung over her shoulder and a rope of licorice curling round her arm. Even so it was plain she was a gentlewoman, anyone could see that by her carriage, by the cut of her fine silk gown.

There was a small child sniveling into the back of that gown. He was the first Hutchinson child I noticed. Only the first. Those Hutchinsons — what a clan of them it seemed coming up the street; eleven children and two spinster cousins and Anne's youngest sister and two menservants, and at the end of this procession, directing the carters along with the cupboard and the baskets and the carved armchair was the head of the family, William Hutchinson, his fair hair beginning to gray above a country-lad face and smart eyes; another tall one, I thought.

I recall someone beside me observing that a march might well be played.

I recall someone else making a rather lewd comment about the clear importance of that bed to this family.

And I recall feeling quite pleased that I was not the one who was to house them till they were settled; the very thought made me weary. I wondered who would.

---

But the Hutchinsons were housing themselves.

The bed was set down on a choice lot across from the Spring Gate where a fine new house had just finished abuilding; only the day before had the glazier done setting the glass in the windows. Ned Hutchinson, the eldest son, of about one-and-twenty, had come out with his uncle ahead of the others and had overseen the work on the house.

All of us had watched it get built.

Before the carpenters and the builders appeared on the lot there was for some time only the broad trench dug for the foundation. A number of children played in the spaded earth on its rim by day; certain servants were rumored to be fornicating at the bottom by night. After the frame was raised Pastor Wilson and Reverend Cotton were twice discovered conversing in the shade of its entry, and for the duration of the brickwork on the chimney several pious mottoes and certain shorter and rather less pious words were written in brick dust on nearby fences.

We women watched the house progress that summer whenever we went to the spring, at least once a day, and when the dwelling was roofed many of us sought shelter from the sun there while awaiting our turns with our buckets; in the shadows of the unfinished great hall we'd cluster together, whispering, resting a moment, passing the dipper from hand to hand.

I think of that often now: people gathering together in Anne's house before we ever knew it as such. Many of us remembered that when she opened the door to us again.

However, on the day I am recalling, that warm September day when the *Griffin* made land, it was not yet Anne's house to me or anyone else I knew. It was simply that new place across from the spring. Sam Cole, the brewer and innkeeper next door, referred to it as The Other Palace at first. It is indeed a larger house than most and certainly as fine a one as the Winthrops' home directly opposite it on the High Street. Sam Cole may have been making comparisons with the Coddingtons' grand house, the only brick one in town, or with someone else's, but I doubt it.

The Other Palace.

That, I think, is the first bit of landing-talk I heard about the Hutchinsons.

Landing-talk begins directly after a ship sets down new neighbors in our midst and lasts about a fortnight, is sometimes reliable, often not, and can't be helped, I suppose, in a wilderness town of some thousand-odd souls such as ours. After living here perhaps two or three summers of ships and landings I grew to pay it less heed but I do recall some of the landing-talk about Anne and her family.

For whatever it may be worth:

They no sooner set foot here than two of their children up and got lost and *"Mary-Sammy-Mary-Sammy"* was all a body could hear that day, the street turned jackanapes with *"Mary-Sammy-Mary-Sammy";* Heaven help us if any more of them get lost . . . how many *are* there?

The sound of a woman sobbing softly was heard at night during the first week through an open casement on the first story where a candle flame streaked slowly back and forth behind the glass.

Mistress Hutchinson's fetching young sister Kit, why she'd soon find herself a husband, indeed she would, but those spinster cousins, speaking-of-course-with-all-charity, noses like turnips they have and those *chins*.

Master Hutchinson was not gentry but was richer than most gentry, richer than Winthrop, who left Suffolk in debt; a prosperous cloth merchant, Hutchinson, with an eye to the main chance. His people? From Alford in Lincolnshire, the Wardalls knew them there, they say his grandfather was mayor of Lincoln Town.

Mistress Hutchinson was a Marbury before her marriage, gentry but low gentry, dusty coats-of-arms and Oxford for her brothers and not much money to speak of; her father, a cleric, was vicar of Alford parish some years, then there was some trouble, retired, moved, raised roses, went to London, I think that's what she said.

She's forty if she's a day and if he's not close to fifty the sea's not close to land and that's the truth of it.

The two of them were seen strolling about their lot very late one unbearably hot night, hardly visible, just the white blur of his shirt and her long shift leaning together in the dark.

What a bonny family they look to be, merry as crickets all, they fill two benches at meeting, ah look at them.

She helped the midwife in Alford a good deal, she did, or is that backwards said? The midwife helped her a good deal indeed, fourteen babes she bore, three she buried.

How galling for John Winthrop, sometime squire of Groton Hall in Suffolk, to have to live across the street from that tradesman's son who prospers all he touches — Hutchinson bought fifty acres in Dorchester, six hundred in Braintree, he means to bid on Taylor's Island and invest in Bendall's Dock, no fool he.

Of course he must want to make a sizable donation to the Boston Latin School and the new Fort; has he been asked, why not, see to it. At once.

She reads, she keeps a journal, seen her jotting while she's got the babe to breast, why aboard the *Griffin* she talked Scripture like a scholar with that skinny new minister Symmes, put his nose right out of joint that did.

Chamber pots: the Hutchinsons, it was said, had ballasted the *Griffin* with them, it was said they owned a dozen, it was said they owned two dozen, it was said the pots were painted with posies, what frivol, it was said.

They know the Reverend Cotton from home, went to his church in English Boston often as they could, 'twas why they came, for his sake.

They knew him not at all; they knew him slight at best.

The Hutchinsons came for religious reasons.

The Hutchinsons came for merchantry reasons.

They came for a mingling of these reasons or not a one of them.

It all depended upon who was giving out the landing-talk.

The next time I remember seeing Anne she was standing on her roof beating the devil out of her chimney.

When I rounded the corner of the High Street and drew nearer on my way to the spring I saw that she was not exactly beating it; she was swinging a broom against it with the deliberate even strokes of a man playing windball in the open fields. She directed her aim at the top row of bricks ringing the chimney where the mortar must have come loose. Her knees clasped the ridgepole and each foot was wedged between strips of shingling as if she were standing up in the saddle, keeping herself balanced at that rather unnerving height. By the time I had reached the Spring Gate across the way I could hear the *plink-plink-plink* of a brick tumbling along the slant of the roof, then a thud as it hit the packed earth by the house.

I have seen men trimming off chimneys before loose pieces could fall on someone below, I have seen cottage women up on their roofs mending thatch, but I had never before seen a gentlewoman dressed to call on Margaret Winthrop in a Lincoln green silk gown astride the sharp peak of a two-and-a-half-story house with her skirts hiked up and her cuffs turned back and her safety in some question, doing the task of a bricklayer's second assistant-journeyman.

This was not passing without notice in the High Street.

Several passersby had halted. Sam Cole stood staring from the gate of his inn next door. Dick Brackett leaned on his backlot fence near the half-built jail. As I turned to the spring I saw my friend Mary Dyer standing stock-still by the trough, shading her eyes with her hand, her pail tilting and her fresh-drawn water trickling away into the dirt.

Anne batted one last brick over the eaves, sneezed, and

began to ease herself down the steep roof to a ladder laid against the wall. There was a brief flash of pale stockings and undershift.

At precisely the same moment Dick Brackett raced across his lot and Sam Cole rushed down his path, their arms outstretched, palms up, eyes fixed on Anne as if to catch her. Oblivious, she climbed down the ladder, skirts billowing, and alighted on the ground, still gazing up at the chimney. Sam Cole and Dick Brackett came to an abrupt halt within a rod of each other, panting, just outside her gate, while five or six Hutchinson children darted forward to collect the bricks and mortar chips.

"Keep the one that almost crowned you, Willie," Anne called to the smallest lad. "A near thing that was, we'll show your father."

She turned round then, looking a bit startled as she noticed the onlookers at her gate for the first time. She nodded politely to everyone, her smile faintly puzzled, scooped up her small son and vanished into the house. She appeared completely unaware that she had done anything extraordinary, unseemly, uncommon.

It was only after I came to know Anne that I realized she was nearly always unaware of such things. She seldom took time to measure the impression she made on those around her.

Unlike her husband.

I shall not soon forget the shaft of blue that shot, with a crack like that from a gun, across the packed earth of the High Street just as I was passing the Hutchinsons' house the next Market Day. It was so sudden I jumped in my shoes, pulled up short. Everyone else in the road had jerked to a dead stop. Hounds yelped. Chickens flapped and squawked, frightened, on the run.

It was a moment before anyone realized what it was: a wide bolt of brilliant blue silk that had unfurled, swift and surprisingly radiant, in our path, and lay shimmering like water in the dust.

It was another moment before I saw the eldest Hutchinson lad, Ned, holding one end of the bolt in his hands, shaking his head as he begged our pardon and went to fetch his brothers' help.

His brothers were otherwise occupied. The two next in age to Ned, young men both, had just broken open a crate that had stood in plain view by their gatepost for a week, still marked from the ship's hold: GRIFFIN — HUTCHINSON — HOLLAND CLOTH. The lads were shouldering a thick bolt of burgundy fabric which slipped and twisted in their grasp, so that several yards of it rolled down and swung between them like a signboard as they slowly carried the bolt past the house and round the corner.

Either the Hutchinson lads were remarkably clumsy, or their father had given them remarkably clever instructions.

I vaguely suspected the latter.

Now, knowing Will Hutchinson as I do, I definitely suspect the latter.

That happened to be midmorning of a Thursday Market Day, when the High Street is milling with folk on their way to the marketplace with coinage or credit to hand, as I had been. People aplenty were there to lean over the silk in admiration, offering to help shake it out, peering into the open crate while they were about it, receiving a quiet word of greeting from Master Hutchinson himself, who stood by, entirely composed, as his two eldest sons rebolted the spilled cloth. Soon enough a number of marketers were in the shop built onto the side of the new house.

William Hutchinson, with a silent flourish that seemed mere chance, had announced to Boston that his door was open for commerce.

Open, airy, festive it was inside too. Fine fabric is a weakness of mine, and it led me into the shop where swags of cloth hung like banners in a palace or a pageant, over the rafters, from the beams, floating just above my head, a breeze from the high windows rustling the swags and sunlight ribboned across the colors: plum, claret, almond, periwinkle, cream. The crush in the shop had grown. I tarried near the bolts of linen, loitered by a roll of twilled broadcloth, was trapped temporarily between the muslin and the baize with Mary Dyer, who had been draping herself in some scarlet silk lining, and flushed. Fey, blond, delicate Mary, she always looked younger than her twenty-six years, and at that moment seemed a tousled child caught trying on her mother's clothes. She was a Londoner used to an array of shops and goods, and her blue eyes were at once homesick and devilishly delighted, particularly as we watched John Winthrop smiling, allowing a quantity of sarsenet silk to ripple over his arm before he told the clerk to parcel some, in black, for his Margaret.

I decided it would be wise for me to leave before sending myself into debt and chose a small measure of lawn, enough to contrive a collar and a handkerchief, and, as I paid the clerk-tailor, Will Hutchinson appeared at my elbow, folded the cloth into a neat square himself, and laid it in my hand, thanking me for my patronage.

He'll fare well here, I recall thinking as I made my way to the door, at the same time thinking over what I could and could not afford at market after this little frivol of mine: no candles this week, half as much bread, that sort of thinking.

Which is partly why I trod on that minister.

I was paying more heed to my own thoughts than I was to my step, though I must say he was crouching directly on the doorsill, craning his neck as if to peer inside without being noticed. He begged my pardon. I begged his. He begged mine again. By that time I had recognized him as that stringy new minister who had come on the *Griffin*, bound for the Charlestown congregation. Symmes, that was his name.

Odd man. I glanced back at him from the road.

He was still hanging about the crowded shop but he was no longer crouching, no longer alone. He was standing with John Winthrop, and as he talked Symmes kept smoothing over and over the same spot on his black cloak while his other hand lifted, pointing, at Anne's house.

Watching them gave me a strange feeling even then.


Bombazine.

That is the next clear word I connect with Anne.

There had been some other words about her, some mutterings when William Hutchinson was churched without his wife, publicly welcomed into the membership of the Boston congregation and the company of Visible Saints, his distant and preoccupied countenance strangely devoid of the pious pleasure most people display on such occasions. Church membership means, on the spiritual level, that one has shown outward signs of sanctification, election, salvation; on the practical level, it means a man may vote. It means a certain standing in the community. It means a certain approval. It meant something that Mistress Hutchinson's churching was delayed. There were rumors that the Reverend Mr. Symmes had requested the delay, having doubts about her doctrinal opinions ever since she had questioned him about a sermon he had preached aboard the *Griffin* during their crossing. There were rumors her opinions were unsound.

But these were only rustlings, blurred whisperings, which passed quickly and were never plain and were only recalled long afterward.

The delay was brief. The Reverend Mr. John Cotton, Anne's friend and counselor from home, as Teacher of Boston Church, and the Reverend Mr. John Wilson, Pastor of Boston Church, examined her thoroughly in private session, as was the custom with women, and found her opinions sound indeed. And so came the Sabbath day when everyone talked of bombazine.

It was on the first of November and the old Feast of All Saints after Arthur Perry had marched through town sounding the drum that calls us to Divine Worship, and everyone in Boston, save the infirm and the dying, tramped down the Great Street and into the meeting house. It was after morning prayers and the first sermon and the first exercise in response to the sermon and *O give thanks unto the Lord because that good is He* — the dreadfully tuneless singing our voices render the psalms, unaccompanied by any worldly unscriptural instrument and lined out by a tone-deaf deacon — after the benediction and the pause for noonday dinner and after the opening of afternoon worship and prayers and the second sermon and exercise and collection and the turning of the large hourglass by the deacons' bench eight times, we were asked to welcome Sister Anne Hutchinson into the bosom of the congregation.

I remember watching her walk down the aisle of that great thatched barn of a meeting house, the late afternoon sun catching in its shiplike rigging of rafters and beams, her step brisk, back straight. The Reverend John Cotton awaited her beneath the pulpit, smiling; this was, in a way, a greeting for a beloved pupil, as Anne had spent many hours studying theology with him in England, following his emphasis on a Gospel of God's love and mercy, offering hope for those who would have faith and humble themselves rather than rely upon their own strenuous works. As he held out his hands in blessing Cotton looked to be a generation older than Anne, rather than a few years; his pale hair, silvering now, wisped like spun sugar round his head, his small stature and large girth, flushed pouchy face, the very roundness of him made him seem an aged cherub. And he preached like an angel; even I could listen to him and find myself caught up in that voice, that phrasing, those words. He was called silver-tongued, golden-tongued, before he was thirty. He was famed throughout East Anglia, drew crowds, packed St. Botolph's. He was sought by the Archbishop's men but escaped to a ship and the lantern in St. Botolph's tower went out. He was welcoming Anne into a new church that day, his church, with joy.

Flanked by the elders and magistrates, Mr. Cotton gave Anne his blessing and formal welcome into the church, and then the members rose one by one in order of social rank to file past Anne and give her greeting while the rest of us sat in our places toward the back and looked on.

There she stood before all of Boston in her grand gown of twilled bombazine, fragile tiffany silk at throat and wrists, looking pleased and tall and centered within her circle of skirts, standing there in her quiet finery, smiling and being smiled upon, receiving and giving two hundred-odd times the right hand of fellowship.

Whatever trouble there had been was clearly past.

Phillip Ratcliffe, as you may have heard, was, for speaking against the ministers, banished, whipped, fined forty shillings, and sentenced to have both ears stricken from his head.

Mary Oliver, for speaking against the ministers, and Robert Shorthouse, for speaking against the magistrates, were hailed before the court, censured, and set to stand in a public place with their tongues in cleft sticks.

Anne Hutchinson, for disagreeing with the point of a minister's sermon, was not admitted to Boston Church until her beliefs were particularly scrutinized and determined sound.

And the matter was forgotten for three years.

*I* should have seen it coming on sooner.

There were signs enough; now they make a pattern so plain I can almost trace it with my finger on the darkness that hangs over my bed. Now I can; not then.

But signs there were, and warnings. One that still wakes me in the night, has waked me just now, came only last April. Less than a year ago that was, the spring before the first trial. Last April. That frightful afternoon Maggie Hett threw her own baby down the marketplace well.

I remember the crowd and the breathing silence after the screams and Maggie crouched on the well's rim, her eyes a scorching blue. Someone ran for the Pastor, someone ran for her husband, some tried to lift her down. She reared back sharp at that, grabbed onto the ropes, kicking, and swung off the rim, hanging there till we all dropped back a pace, her gaze burning into us all the while. No one tried to come near her after that.

"Certain 'tis certain," she said, distinct and calm. "Certain I be damned now."

Her eyes were clear; then clouded. They darkened suddenly with such terror that for a moment I could not imagine what she beheld as she gazed out over our heads, not till I heard the murmur run through the crowd: *Pastor coming, her husband away from home, Pastor Wilson has come.* She must have seen the fringe of the crowd part for him, seen it unbraiding before him, seen that steady flow of black robes past aprons and doublets and smocks and skirts. From a distance the Pastor's ashen hair, struck by sun and sea breeze, seemed to smoke from his head. For a moment the wind lifted his wide sleeves, winglike, as he bore down upon the well. Closer, half-running and short of breath, he looked fleshy, dusty, sweat-streaked, his round face as rough and moist and red as a hound's tongue.

"Goodwife Hett! In the name of Our Lord I say come down."

Maggie made no move.

"Come down, let us see to the babe."

"Drowned," said Maggie.

"Down! For the babe's sake, for the sake of your soul."

"I had to know," she said, clear, precise.

"Goody Hett, hear me."

"Damned. Saved. Which one."

"I command you."

"Had to be certain which, now 'tis."

"Woman! Turn from this wickedness, this is unclean, this is of Satan, this monstrous sin, flesh drowning one's own flesh."

Several people near me were making small circles in the air with thumb and forefinger, circles to the left, the sign against evil. Many, I knew, would not touch her now.

Wilson steppped toward her suddenly; reached for her. She spun from him, veered off balance, arms spread, flailing. A sound like the whir of a spinning wheel rose from the crowd.

Before she'd righted herself, grabbing the ropes and gripping them tight, I was stealing off toward the far side of the well. She'd never come down for Pastor Wilson, unlikely it was she'd come down even for beloved Reverend Cotton had he been there, unlikely she'd come down for anyone at all, but perhaps if she saw a face she'd trusted she'd not lose herself entirely; I'd seen her through a birthing long and hard, she might remember.

". . . a mother drowning her own child to seek — nay, ensure, her own damnation." Pastor Wilson turned to the crowd as I neared the well. "Take you all a lesson from this abomination, how weak we are, what easy prey . . ."

Standing on the well's rim, Maggie bent her head and wept within a sheet of fair hair that had fallen down round her face, her hand strung limp through the ropes like a pale leaf that had blown and caught there.

"Let us pray. Oh Lord to whom vengeance belongeth, show Thyself. Lord, how long shall the wicked triumph . . ."

Kneeling by the well's far side, eyes just above the rim, I saw: far-off faces, knucklelike rows of them massed together; the loose black cloth of Wilson's gown snapping like a flag in the wind as it hung from his outstretched arm, forefinger jabbing air. The well ropes, twisted, strips of sky between. Tangled within the ropes, Maggie's arm, green-sleeved, the cloth split at the seam, her hand raw with rope burns, scrapes. And then a blue sleeve reaching across faces, sky, arms; next to the green one a blue sleeve of fine cloth, familiar long-fingered hand covering the limp one caught in the ropes.

"Blazes!" I heard Anne's voice mutter, and the sound of shoes slipping on the moss-covered well stones.

A moment later I could see her sitting next to Maggie on the well's rim, heard her voice again, low, steady, mingling with Maggie's, and beyond that a continuous rustling from the crowd and the rumbling of the Pastor's prayers. And another sound, one I could not place at first. A faint mewing sound close by. Odd overtone to it like an echo. Rising, leaning closer, squinting down the shaft, *there:* the babe. Alive, bless God, red-faced, cupped in the bucket above the water. Dazed, no doubt, but alive and lacking signs of hurt so far as

I could see; the tightly bound swaddling clothes had saved him.

My eyes met Anne's over the well. I pointed down the shaft. She looked, eyes widening, looked again. For an instant she paused, casting a glance at Maggie; her hand made a flat palm-down motion: wait. She turned, her arm still round Maggie, her voice beginning that low steady undertone again, and began easing the both of them off the well's rim: green gown, blue gown wavering there, straightening up, one lower than the other for a moment, halting, suddenly still, then moving again, slowly moving off together, the blue and green meshing with the crowd.

I reached out for the well rope and pulled.

When I lifted the baby from the bucket and held him up, him bellowing heartily by then, there was a wordless sweep through the crowd and then, almost like a chant, over and over: *God be praised God be . . .*

Pastor Wilson began speaking again, explaining the sign, as I ducked off with the infant in my arms. Few followed, most stayed, it was expected. Even so, I dodged down the paths and turnings I knew from getting quick to childbeds, so as to lose those plucking fingers, those curious eyes.

Round a corner, across a lot, and I was in the Mylne Lane, slowing my pace, keeping back, watching Anne walk Maggie along. Let her get home first, inside, get her home. Maggie was all fair hair and trailing skirts, hair down, hem down, green linsey-woolsey spilling into the lane; just a frightened gawk of a lass she looked of a sudden. And Anne: taller, much taller, with that elegant bearing of hers, part breeding, part backache, striding on in her fine midnight-blue gown, perfect cut, perfect collar and cuffs of the best cream lawn, but for all that what was just as striking was the skirts hitched up in three places and held with wooden pegs, showing undershift and shins and the watermarks on the fine cloth and the sleeves shoved above the elbow and the dark hair uncovered, snatched up into a knot atop her head, and some unidentifiable piece of linen dangling from her fingers, quite forgotten. She could have just stepped away from a carriage or a washtub.

We were almost to the house when the infant in my arms began to cry again and Maggie heard, turned, broke. In the lane, in the mud, she knelt and held out her arms for the child and rocked him to her, sobbing, asking us and herself and God how she could have done this thing, what had come over her, while we stood round about her, tenting her in with our skirts.

"My child my God my child." Maggie bowed her head. "Ah what's happened. Don't let Pastor come, please not him, Mr. Cotton maybe later, not Pastor, dear God please."

We let her lean into our knees.

"Unregenerate Maggie, how poor my soul's worth. Pastor kept warning warning warning. Unregenerate, poor, impoverished spiritual estate. Not enough works, good works, not at Sabbath meeting often enough, evening prayers, morning prayers, not enough, examination of conscience, visiting the sick, not enough, like my father nothing ever enough."

She couldn't go regular to meeting, she was ill: three miscarryings, then this child, ill all through the bearing and birthing and afterward as well.

"All this winter I brooded over what Pastor had said and said and said, how I lacked outward signs of santification, how each miscarrying was a sign of my spiritual lack, his words they came to own me, to sit on my chest at night."

There were others he had pushed too hard like this; Anne and I and Jane had all heard this from other mouths, other times; much the same, much gasped out in pain, in fear.

"After a while I didn't know whose face I'd see when I looked in the well. A damned one, a saved one, sanctified, unregenerate, what, whose? A face swam in the water but what was it, he wouldn't say, not knowing was worse since the babe came, what did he have for a mother then?"

Some are weaker than others and cannot bear as much: if

I as a midwife know this simple truth, why I be damned if a minister shouldn't know it, him cupping in his fingers souls more fragile than the neck of a birthing babe I hold and guide.

"I know what I've done, what I've tried to do." Maggie looked up at us. "The shame of it, dear Lord, child, my little one, let me get thee home."

We got her inside, got her to bed. I saw that Anne bolted the door but said nothing. By the time I'd seen to the baby, finding no great hurt beyond two bruises on him, and the fire was stirred, and the kettle was swung over the hearth, we could hear the sound of people, many people, all around the house.

Anne was silent, white, standing at the shuttered windows.

There was a rapping at the door.

"Ah dear God, what will they do to me?" Maggie wept.

The rapping came again.

"They'll take my babe from me, they will."

"They'll not," said Anne, sharp.

She didn't move, turn. The knocking on the door continued as I went to Maggie, trying to quiet her, quiet the child. Anne stood for a moment more by the shutters, very still, tensed, frowning. She steepled her fingers together, touched them to her chin, once, twice, lightly; and crossed to the entry and opened the door.

All at once a rush of noise flooded the house: voices, boots, shuffling, shouts. Pastor Wilson stepped forward, framed by the door.

"I am come for Goodwife Hett," he said.

Anne neither spoke nor moved from the doorway. I could see Wilson squinting past her shoulder; squinting past his were as many faces as could jam a doorframe, trying to see the weeping woman, the child.

"I am come for Margaret Hett," Wilson said, an edge on his voice.

"The constable is with you then, sir?" said Anne. "With a writ."

John Winthrop appeared at Wilson's side. I saw the long flaring nose, the pale agate eyes. For a moment nothing was to be heard but the shuffling of feet and a log snapping on the fire, while Winthrop stared about. He was a magistrate, could order what he wished. I felt Maggie coil against me.

"A case of distraction, female distraction . . ." The breath whistled down Winthrop's nose like wind down an elegant staircase. "The constable likes not to enter into these matters. Pastor Wilson has leave to exercise the proper authority, this has again become a spiritual matter. No writ necessary. Good night, madam."

With the air of a man who has stooped beneath him, Winthrop withdrew his narrow face from the doorway; Wilson's fleshy one seemed to fill it.

"Leave me to her then, she must be exhorted, her soul's in peril."

Anne said nothing.

"She is tainted," said Wilson.

"She is distracted."

"Preparative sorrow is but a beginning, she needs exhortation."

"She needs rest."

"She must hear me."

"Look on her, sir, she's not able to hear anyone tonight."

"It would greatly benefit all to exhort her in public."

"It would tear her in two."

"You deprive the community."

"I take that upon myself."

"If she again resorts to Satan, you not leaving her a minister . . ."

"I take that upon myself as well."

"I warned her," said Wilson.

"Indeed you did."

There was a long silence that made me uneasy.

"I warned you," Wilson said at last.

"Good night, sir."

"I warn you now."

"Good night, sir."

They stood there for a moment, not speaking. I saw the look he cast her, so long and unblinking, so dark, it was if he meant to stamp something on her face with his eyes.

I felt mightily afraid for Anne in that moment, as if a great wind had begun blowing through the house, sweeping with it ladles and shoes and sheets and everything we knew.

But only for a moment.

In the next moment the door was bolted again. The brew on the hearth came to boil and the betty-lamps were kindled and the room filled with warmth. I watched Anne straddling a stool by the bedside, amber light curling on her shoulder like a cat, head back in a laugh, trying to sing in her awful voice so as to get Maggie singing in her lovely one.

Nothing could happen, I thought. Not to her.

Not to Anne.

*T*hat hole in the window disturbs me.

Other than that I think her house looks much the same as ever. It will be some time before the gate hangs crooked and things turn shabby, before weeds grow up in the path. But no doubt someone will purchase it soon enough and there will be no shabbiness, there will be no weeds.

I do not like to think of stones being cast at Anne's windows. Nor do I like to think of another woman living in her house.

But I do think of these things, when I go to the spring, the market, the hills; whenever I must pass that lot, that house. Her house: people still point it out. What they say I know not, but in her time Anne Hutchinson's house was pointed out to visitors with respect, with — pardon the word — pride. To her house and to her meetings came colony treasurers, magistrates, captains of the militia, and even Sir Harry Vane, our governor that year. To her house, to her meetings, came town selectmen, prosperous merchants, church deacons, widows and wives, and came as well carters, fishermen, the schoolmaster, the seamstress and the sawyer, the hog-reeve, the ferrymaster.

To her house quite lately came someone who pried back the shutters so that a stone could spin through the glass windowpanes and God's Body I want to know who.

---

Those windows had a way of glimmering at you through the dimming mists of candlelighting time, especially when there was a meeting, and there was a meeting every week, one night a week for two years. The candle beam within would cast a bar of brightness across the top of that window and afterward a spill of light would come from the doorway and the lanterns we had fetched along, all those lanterns, would wink and bob on the darkness outside in the street.

Comfortable it was to be there.

Comfortable to be standing in the dust or mud or snow some night in August, March, January, your lantern swinging from your fingers and all about you, hanging on the night air, the scents of tallow and woodsmoke and pitch, and the voices of people you knew well or scarce knew at all and little it mattered which.

Comforting to stand with a cluster of friends, a breeze on your face as you watched chimney sparks spin like fireflies off into the sky, and waving, and calling and hearing back again and again, distant and sweet and clear *good night-good night-good night* . . .

At the time I never thought to count but I do think there must have been fifty or sixty of us and sometimes as many as eighty — eighty work-weary grown folk lingering in the street with our nodding lanterns like children trying to postpone bedtime.

I stood there so many times.

I remember standing there last April: only a year ago.

The third week in April: the evening mild, the meeting over, the house filled with people and the street bobbing with lights — it was the last of those evenings that seemed comforting, perpetual, safe. I remember it quite particularly. I remember standing in the Hutchinsons' entry, talking with Mary Dyer about mustard seeds. There was a new candle in my lantern and a smell of lilac from the garden and the murmur of voices all around us.

As always Anne was still in the great hall — people stayed

to talk long after a meeting ended. She was an easy one to catch sight of in the crowded room because of her height: when I glanced from the entry into the great hall I could see the top of her head at once, then a slice of green gown, her lanky frame leaned up against the end of the long trestle table; her eyes — remarkable gray eyes in an unremarkable angular face — were serious, concentrated on an elderly man talking to her; then he let go her hand, I caught her gaze and she smiled, beginning to ease her way toward us.

Behind her the low-beamed chamber was flushed with firelight, candlelight, rippling with voices and laughter, while shadows went streaming like spirits up the whitewashed walls, across the smoke-stained ceiling. By the hearth, amidst the clutter of trivets and andirons, a knot of people stood talking, the men emptying their pipes; more had gathered by the court cupboard, that great carved crouching thing, a prune-colored heirloom and a chunk of England, its array of pewter touched with amber from the fire. There, his hand on a tankard, stood Will Hutchinson.

". . . on my way home, he was a young lad, never saw him before," he was saying, "And there he was, no greeting, no introduction, falling into step with me, sharing his lantern, coming right to it: 'Sir,' he says, 'if you'd go along with me tonight I'll bring you to a woman that teaches better Gospel than any of your blackcoats at a university, a woman of another spirit entirely she is, with revelations of things to come . . .' "

Anne raised an eyebrow.

" 'For my part,' he goes on, 'I'd rather hear such a one than any of your blackcoat scholars. They preach to impress one another, she talks to make things plain. They tell terrors, she tells love. The people have begun to call her a prophetess raised up of God, and I cannot say that nay. If you would but come with me, if you could but meet her once you would know with your own soul what I'm telling.' He never did ask my name, so intent he was on urging me, hastening me — to my own wife."

"I sent him," said Anne, amidst the laughter. "Supper was getting cold."

"Can't recall seeing him there, that's what's odd. Do you know who he could be, Nan?"

Anne shook her head.

"These tales," she said. "These . . . fables. How do they begin, they make me uneasy. Next they'll be saying that one night a week behind closed doors, before an intimate gathering of perhaps . . . two thousand, that merchant's wife turns water into wine. Or rather, this being Boston, she turns wine into water."

And there was more laughter, more pipes filled as the candles burned down.

The house was still half-full when a lad of no more than ten skidded into the room, his eyes wide, gaze darting about, announcing in a cracked whistle of a voice that there was an urgent call for Mistress Hutchinson and Goodwife Benedict to come at once, Midwife Hawkins could not be found, come at once with him.

That's the way of it, I'm well used to it, as was Anne. We reached down our cloaks, lit our lanterns. I told the lad to run and fetch my midwifery basket with its medicinal vials, scissors, forceps, all manner of necessities, but he looked at me queer and said he must take us to the house himself, and directly, so he was commanded, not to go anywhere else nor let us out of his sight.

We went off through the dark, the lad's lantern jouncing up ahead of us, the moon blinking through the fence slats as we trudged up the sloping lane past the burying ground.

Here and there a window glowed amber, but most of Boston was asleep by now; it was past curfew. I could feel the damp air in my head, my chest. I could hear Anne's quick breathing. Both of us, I knew, were wondering who had been brought to childbed that night; none I could think of were due, it would be an early birthing then. The lad, running ahead. did not answer when we called questions to him. Odd boy; I couldn't place his face. He might have been a servant's child: the punch-holes in his lantern were merely random sprinklings of light, not a design that signified its owner.

We veered right, the grade steepening as we neared Sudbury End and the Reverend John Cotton's house rose before us.

"Sarah Cotton?" Anne said. "It couldn't be."

Unless she was ill, miscarrying, something wrong we hadn't known. In any case the windows of her house were lit, scattering diamond-shaped slivers of light across the front lot, while the lad's lantern wobbled by the gatepost. We rushed up the path.

The door opened, just a hand's width. Sarah Cotton drew us inside, her lips tight, her eyes jumping beyond us. She shut the door so swiftly it nearly caught my cloak. Her greeting was short, sharp, whispered. Her fingers bore into my arm, even as she slipped our cloaks from our shoulders, and then she was leading me to the stair, walking with me, walking fast, nearly marching me along.

I turned to see if Anne was behind me; I turned, and saw them all at once.

Just beyond the entry in the great hall of the house stood a row of silent men. Their black clothing seemed to soak up the light from the hearth and the candles behind them. Their hands were folded. Their white forked neckbands stood out stiff from their throats. They seemed not to move. Eleven of them. Every minister in the Bay Colony gathered there. Every pair of eyes, in that moment, fixed on me. I felt the shock, like another body slamming into mine, that Anne must have known an instant earlier. For there she was, standing before them. Their eyes shifted back to her. She was the one they were waiting for.

Sarah Cotton was hastening me up the stairs, our feet skimming the steps, turning sharp on the wedged landing, breathless, our heels clacking higher, fast through the passageway above, and into a small upper chamber.

"Forgive me, Goody Benedict," Sarah Cotton murmured.

Behind me the door was shut, bolted. I was alone. The narrow bed was empty. In the dim room nothing stirred. Vague shapes sat in the moonlight: a chest, a stool, a pair of barrels. Something swept the top of my head: a string of dried peppers, a remnant of last winter's stores. The only light in the room came from the moon, carved hard and clear against the night sky, and from the floor: strips of light where the boards did not meet close together. As a child sent early to bed I used to fix my eyes on those runners of light we all remember, glimmering in our bedchambers as if the fairies had trailed them there, and I would gaze at them until I fell asleep. As an old woman locked in a strange room under odd circumstances I fixed my eyes on the bright floorcracks and watched them glow, suddenly vanish, glow again, dim, glow. The changes were not my aging eyesight. The changes were not my fancy. Nothing of the kind. There was a rumbling of voices and boots beneath me. Without any shame or hesitation I knelt down and put my eye to the largest crack.

I found myself crouching above the great hall of John Cotton's house — at least five floorboards' worth — over a corner of the room. Likely they'd put me in there because the main upper chamber was directly over it and the other small ones were unheated. Sarah Cotton had a kindly heart; a shoulder of the great chimney thrust up through this room, warming me as I peered down.

Like dark fish in a pond they were moving below me. A sweep of black cloth, a sleeve, a back. Creaks, coughs, benches scraping: still arranging themselves. Directly beneath me was the flat shine of polished oak near firelight: a corner of the long trestle table. A hand, thin and blue-veined, was setting down quill, sandcaster, inkpot, paper. A circlet of black suddenly appeared, as if hanging just below me. I was looking down on the head of a minister: his black silken skullcap, white hair floating out round it radiant from the firelight. Another minister joined him at the corner of the table, I could see another, fleshier, freckled hand. The rest were taking their places beyond my view, and Anne, I supposed, must be at the other end of the table, the end I could not see. All at once the scrapings and rumblings ceased, as if on signal. Silence, then: a long thrumming silence. And as abruptly as it had begun it was blown from the room by the roar of a voice; I flinched above it.

"You were invited, Mistress Hutchinson, to answer to reports that you condemn our ministry."

That bellow of a voice came from Hugh Peter, minister of Salem, I was certain: a man I have heard as a visiting preacher on Lecture Day, a man I have never known to speak lower than a shout. I could see his arm, a muscular one, his hand furred with dark hair pointing, curling back into a fist.

"I put it directly, why do you cast aspersions on the ministers of this country?"

A pause.

No reply.

"I think perhaps we might give our guest a few moments to recover from this unexpected summons," came the gentle voice of John Cotton. "We are not gathered here, after all, to conduct an inquisition, are we, only to clarify certain points about Mistress Hutchinson's meetings. May I say, reverend brothers, that I myself recommended that she attend the women's neighborhood prayer meetings, such as they were, soon after she arrived in Boston."

"And there lies the root of the trouble." That was the curdled-milk tones of Anne's old enemy, Zachariah Symmes. "Those neighborly conventicles were in a disgraceful state long before Mistress Hutchinson joined them. Prayer meetings they were not, female gossip feasts is all they were."

"Just so." Cotton went smoothly on. "And we were all deeply pleased when Mistress Hutchinson opened her large and commodious house to these meetings and raised them to a level of enlightenment we never thought to see."

"And more." Down the table, our friend Elder Leverett spoke. "Mistress Hutchinson's meetings reached out to the women who cannot attend Divine Worship — and we notice each Sabbath what a number they are — women ill, or with child, or in childbed, or unable, otherwise confined by household obligations."

"The women trust her." Deacon Coggeshall spoke from the table's far end. "They'll ask her to explain knotty points in Scripture they fear to ask us. They'll turn to another woman. Indeed Mistress Hutchinson averted a near catastrophe at the well only a few days past . . . with Pastor Wilson's help . . . of course."

There was a strained silence. John Cotton had orchestrated his support well; perhaps too well.

"Come, gentlemen, are you attempting to have Mistress Hutchinson elected governor of the colony? Knighted perhaps?" Surely that was the acidic wit of Ipswich's Pastor Ward. "If all were well I wouldn't have been obliged to ride thirty miles. I was assured this was an urgent matter."

"All is *not* well, I tell you." A blast of a voice made me jump; Thomas Weld of Roxbury rose, the sweep of his sleeve darkening the floor-crack for an instant. Then the light returned, showing an empty place at the table below. His voice, deep and hoarse, blew like a wind of splinters through the room. "There is a canker growing here and we cannot dose it with sugar-water — nay! Hear me, hear me well. Mistress Hutchinson, do you deny that for more than a year your meetings have grown from simple neighborhood prayer meetings for the women into large gatherings for men and women, that you invite some of the most powerful and wealthy political men in the colony to some of these gatherings?"

In the silence there was a rustle of skirts, a strangely feminine sound after that deep voice, that heavy stride. She must have stood up; I could see the heads below me turning, tilting.

"Speak up, Mistress Hutchinson, open your mind to us plainly else you disgrace your teacher Reverend Mr. Cotton, who beseeched us to allow you a word in your own behalf. Do you deny the presence of these men at your meetings?"

"No sir. I do not discriminate."

There was a faint hum of laughter below. I smiled in the dark. "But sir, I invite no one. All are welcome, the door is left open. That is all."

"Has any minister or elder of the church sanctioned this change?" Weld's shoes creaked as he strode the table's length.

"Aye," Elder Leverett said. "Church membership has nearly doubled since and . . ."

"That is not the point." Weld cut him off. "These meetings of yours, Mistress Hutchinson, began two years ago, just as Pastor Wilson sailed for England on pressing personal business. He was gone a twelve-month, leaving Mr. Cotton in Boston's pulpit and you to your own devices. Now answer me this: In the past year, since Pastor Wilson has returned, have you not disparaged his preaching? Have you not compared it unfavorably with Mr. Cotton's? Have you not, in fact, condemned your own pastor, condemned me, condemned every one of us whom you have heard on Lecture Day excepting only Mr. Cotton and Mr. Wheelwright?"

"I condemn no one," said Anne. "I condemn no one's words. That I do question certain teachings is true. That I see distinctions between certain teachings, that is also true. But condemnation? Nay. You say the meetings used to be gossip feasts . . . ah, then, *then* perhaps you would have found the slander and condemnation you now suspect."

Another faint stir of amusement below.

Then Pastor Wilson's voice, taut and sharp as drawn wire, cut through the sound and the chamber went still.

"I can remain silent no longer. Here is the danger, the very core of it. Mistress Hutchinson is creating divisions amongst us. You find, madam, a difference between my preaching and Mr. Cotton's, do you not? You find a difference between the main of all our preaching and the preaching of two others, do you not?"

A moment passed.

"I do find such a difference," Anne said.

"How dare you meddle in matters of theology? How dare you label us as one sealed with the Holy Spirit, another not? Who *are* you to be passing judgments on us, your ministers, your elders?"

"Not judgments, sir. They are but observations. We all must make observations, I think, else we shall cease to observe, and then we shall be blind leading the blind, is that not so?"

"Observations, judgments . . . with all due respect, madam, you sound like a Jesuit. I for one like not the influence your judgments — or shall I say 'observations' — or perhaps 'dissent' — have over many in this town."

"And yet, the clergy blessed our meeting only a year ago, did I not hear you all say so?"

"A year ago!" Hugh Peter's roar hung in the room below like smoke. "A year ago, madam, you were praising Mr. Cotton's sermons and elucidating them. Now you are disagreeing with Pastor Wilson's sermons and speaking your criticism before large gatherings — I tell you I like not that influence you've gained, I like it not at all."

"Perhaps, sir, if I agreed with Mr. Wilson and praised his sermons before large gatherings, you would like my influence better."

"That is not what I said." The flat of Hugh Peter's palm smacked the table.

Beneath me the quivering halo of white hair, irradiated by the firelight, leaned forward.

"Tell me, Mistress Hutchinson." A frail reedy voice spoke. "Do I preach with the seal of the Spirit? What do you conceive of such a brother as myself?"

"You seek to trick me, Mr. Phillips. I have never heard you preach, as you must know."

Silence again, hands passing over the table, heads together a moment, then apart.

"Gentlemen, gentlemen," came the pale threadlike voice of Newtowne's Pastor Sheperd. "Let us keep sight of what is important here. This gentlewoman is drawing theological differentiations amongst us. She is telling the people of Boston that all of us, excepting two brothers, are preaching nothing but works. Indeed, that is precisely what she is doing. Accusing us of legalism, telling it over and over, drawing false distinctions."

"I see distinctions, I don't draw them," said Anne, an edge to her voice. "I see them because they are there. It would be insulting to you to say otherwise. Each of you does not rattle off by rote the same sermon with the same point, the same interpretation seen from the same angle, each Sabbath Day, all over the Massachusetts Bay Colony."

"You have not addressed yourself to the matter of works and grace, madam. You are on dangerous ground indeed, slandering us by saying all but two of our number are in a covenant of works, and know not how to preach grace. This is what has been reported to us. Do you answer to this charge or nay?"

"I shall answer." Anne's heels rapped the floor. A streak of green swung into my sight: a fold of her skirt and her hand gripping the fold, knuckles white, too white to fit with the calm voice. "Never have I said Pastor Wilson or anyone preaches *only* a covenant of works, all I have said is that to me, as I perceive it, Mr. Cotton and Mr. Wheelwright preach a covenant of grace more clearly. Grace and works." Her fingers opened, then clutched the fold of green cloth again. "Gentlemen, we are caught on that old theological dilemma. As you well know, some ministers emphasize works: outward things, going to church, saying prayers, fasting, sobriety, mortification of the flesh as ways to sanctification. Other ministers say that grace must come first, that first one's heart must feel the presence of God's love, of the Holy Spirit within, and from that presence good works flow naturally, not out of fear, or according to a rulebook, but out of desire. It has seemed to me that Mr. Cotton and Mr. Wheelwright state the importance of grace more emphatically. May I not voice what I observe, in private, in my own home?"

The ministers' voices passed down the table, round the room.

"You do believe in works as well as grace?"

"Of course, sir. In balance. I never said otherwise."

"It is for you only a matter of emphasis?"

"Emphasis, is that all? A thirty-mile ride to carp over emphasis?"

" 'Tis not nearly what we were led to believe."

"The difference between one and another then is not so great."

"The difference, Mistress Hutchinson, put it forward."

"Gentlemen," said Anne. "After the Resurrection and the gift of the Spirit, the Apostles were different men. They heard and saw and spoke in a new way. Some of us, both listeners and speakers, differ in much the same ways. I am a listener. Perhaps my ears are not open to what I ought to hear. Perhaps some of you are not speaking so that I might hear it. It is a point we might debate all night and still find no answer."

The ministers began debating amongst themselves, querulous, some of the voices, the strongest talk coming from the far end of the table out of my sight.

---

43

Down across the floorboards I saw a knothole glittering. I crept toward it, knee by knee, quietly. The board groaned suddenly and squeaked back into place. I froze at the knothole. And found myself staring into a pair of stinging blue eyes that held me fast, as if in a spell. Only in a vague way did I see the florid face, the throbbing vein at the temple of Pastor Wilson, so fixed I was by his glare. I knew he could not see me. I knew it could not have been more than a moment that his eyes stung mine. I knew and yet for an instant I could not move. I understood then what power they had, all of them, even over the likes of me, unchurched, irreverent, inconsistent in belief.

The inquisition seemed to be over. I heard one or two men say they would not be so quick to believe rumors in the future, that the matter was closed, it was not what they had expected, not what they had feared. I heard the door bang shut twice, three times. I heard the scrape of boots and benches, and the shapes beneath me shifted continuously until there was nothing but the dull sheen of firelight on polished wood. More voices, more boots, more *chunk-chunk* of the massive front door swinging to. The candles were snuffed in the chamber below. Sometimes you know that someone is looking at your back without turning round; that is the only way I can explain how I was aware that the chamber beneath me was not completely emptied; it was an uneasy sensation, like knowing one is not alone in the dark.

For a few moments all was still. Then, directly below, there were footsteps. Not Anne's stride. A man's. A poker stirring the fire. A bench creaking.

And then a laugh, a man's laugh, low and dry, scattered about the room like dead leaves. All I could see was a sliver of green silk hovering below me. Anne was still there. She and the stranger.

"You came out of that one unscathed, didn't you? Well. A minister's daughter, they might have known. Yes, you managed well indeed this time." I knew that voice. It had not spoken once during the earlier meeting. And yet he might have been there all the time.

"Your husband must be proud of you, Mistress Hutchinson. Those meetings of yours must be doing wonders for his cloth trade as well."

A pattering of cold laughter.

There was the chink and gurgle of ale being poured, the scrape of a bench pulled in.

"I am grateful to Mr. Cotton for granting me this time alone to speak with you," said John Winthrop. "I have heard you address your meetings on my way past your house; the footpath between your great hall and the Inn is my customary terrain for my evening walks. Indeed I have been arrested by your voice, your words, and have stood there, frankly listening, and to my surprise admiring. Ah 'tis true, 'tis true, you have a way with the people; and a way with the most complex passages in Scripture, the knottiest points of a sermon, what would baffle a conclave of Jesuits let alone simple women . . . ah but you make it all so very simple."

"Not simple, sir. Clear, I hope." Anne said. "I thank you for your kind words."

"Forgive my being somewhat forward, but have you not thought to speak in a public way, at weekly Lecture Days, even in other towns? Nay? Never? But you are gifted, come, you must admit there are special graces given . . ." He paused, spoke softer. "Someone with your gifts should speak from mountain tops. And to multitudes."

He said that last gravely, and the grave voice blended into a silence. I heard a log shift in the grate, a mug set down firm.

"You honor me," Anne said after a while. "Though I think you are too kind. And as it is, all the mountain tops in New England are taken just now."

"You mock me, Mistress Hutchinson."

"Never that. I meant that there are many ministers here in their pulpits and 'tis their office, not mine, to speak to the multitudes."

"You say that with such ease." His voice went on, even, calm. "And yet this colony is torn apart by this controversy, grace versus works, minister against minister — or am I misinformed?"

"Misinformed?" Anne's laugh was dry. "I hadn't expected to find you were being *informed* at all. Ah but *mis*informed, that *is* to be expected."

More polite laughter. Thinner.

"We must avoid the evils of disunity which nearly destroyed the Jamestown settlement in Virginia. Settlements in this wilderness are endangered so mightily from without we cannot allow any perilous divisions within."

Anne's firm step reached the hearthstone.

"This colony does not tear so easily. Jamestown was founded by men in search of riches; they brought no families at first; they came, in the beginning, not to settle but to find gold. We are quite different. We brought our families, all our worldly goods, we have planted and built, and we have settled our land. We are strong enough to bear the weight of more than one opinion; we have differed on various matters from roads to forts to the charter in the past seven years, and not yet split asunder."

"Not yet. But the founders of this colony, the men who built it from a piece of paper, the men who built the meeting house and appointed the ministers — they would find disunity no different from disloyalty."

"You are referring to yourself?"

"There are other powerful men, Dudley, Endicott . . ."

"I know them all."

". . . they can't be pleased with your dissent, are you aware of their views? Are you truly aware of mine?"

"Come, sir, we are neighbors. You and I have observed

each other emptying out chamber pots. It seems unlikely that I should be unaware of your views."

"You refuse to be serious?"

"I am quite serious."

"You must know that I chose Wilson to be pastor when it was all in the offing, the charter, the Bay company. Not Boston's choice, perhaps, the moves amongst the congregation to oust him are well known. Not my first choice. But . . . my choice nonetheless."

"Of course."

"And yet you choose to support the movements in the congregation to replace him. You condemn his opinions . . ."

"Question, not condemn."

"Very well, but to take the part of some poor mad woman against him and before much of the town, as you did a few days past, does that not seem to you a trifle unnecessary in retrospect?"

"I find her madness unnecessary. In retrospect. Sir."

"You shan't be able to take many more risks like that. Harry Vane's term as Governor is nearly over, you know that. He can't protect you once he's out of office. I understand he plans to return to England."

"You have made it uncomfortable for him here."

"He has made it uncomfortable for himself."

In the silence I could hear Winthrop drawing air in through his pipe, could see a crimped edge of the old-fashioned ruff he still wore; it looked oddly decorative against the dimness of the room below.

"I intend to be Governor again in May," he said. "You think me cold, no doubt, most do. But I have suffered these past four years out of power, standing aside, watching others misgovern and misguide this colony. I know it isn't in my nature to win the love of the people as Governor Vane has. And as you have. But their respect, that I shall have back again. That I shall indeed. This colony's needs are as intimately known to me as my own, this colony is, after all, partly my invention, this colony . . . I love it as I never thought possible. When I was a young widower I thought never again could I give affection, share the secrets of my heart . . . and then there was Margaret and it happened so quickly. My poor Margaret, it is still hard for her here, though she says not; she still misses Suffolk, as I thought I would. How I loved it there, how I loved Groton Manor. I remembered for some time each tree, each path; and yet now in my memory it looks too soft, too pale besides Massachusetts. This is the land that is dear to me now. I have given to it, and in full measure . . . my son, my Harry, just entered into manhood, drowned the day we landed here." His voice was shaking. "Child after child born to Margaret in such agony, each buried in this ground so soon after each birth. I have given, and I have been strengthened. It is meant to be so . . . forgive me, I have been too open perhaps."

"Never that. You honor me with your confidence."

"I want you to understand me and understand me well. It is my calling to guide and build this colony, to raise the new Zion, to make it truly a city on a hill. It is an ordained design. I cannot question it, I cannot allow anyone to cross this Divine plan again. And I shall not." His footsteps began crossing the room, slow and deliberate, as if he were marking off property. "I shall let no one oppose me. And you do oppose me. Whenever you oppose Pastor Wilson or Mr. Weld, or any of my ministers, you oppose me. You oppose me by drawing people to yourself so strongly that you create your own faction. You oppose me with your meetings."

"I oppose no one, sir. I speak in private, in my own home. No law governs what I say at my hearthside, only what I speak in public."

"Ah, and you have been most careful and canny of that, have you not? But that distinction alone may not keep you safe forever. Are these meetings really worth the risk to you and your family? In the end what does it all amount to, these gatherings graced by a prayer or two, sermons explained, Scriptural tangles untangled, some fellowship . . . little meetings: at what cost?"

A bench creaked, then a floorboard, with a long slow rustle of skirts. Anne's voice, clear as ice, came from another part of the room.

"I think you have missed what we do," she said, "at our 'little meetings.' They are not political. They are not a faction. They include all who wish to come. They break no law. They are not public. And the meetings are not based upon me, 'tisn't false modesty to say so, you have heard for yourself what they are. The meetings are . . . like a net: the mesh of our thoughts shared aloud, whatever people bring, the comfort, the clarity we find in these times, that is what shapes our gatherings, perhaps our dreams, our very souls, who knows?"

"Maybe so, maybe so. But this is no longer an ordinary neighborhood prayer meeting, as it began. You are . . . you've been referred to . . ."

"As what? Oh come, it can't be so awful. Lucrezia Borgia? Maid Marian?"

"Ah, Boston's wisewoman, for one . . ."

"Foolishness . . ."

"You are a power here, you must know that. Famed for solving spiritual difficulties, more resorted to for counsel than the ministers, so I've heard — why do you look at me like that, 'tisn't nonsense at all, were you laughing?"

"Was I? I hadn't noticed."

"The laws keep you to your little meetings, do they not? Laws against sedition, libel, traducing the ministers. But surely you realize if you would only overlook the small disparities in doctrine, these very small differences with the ministers, these fine fine points — why you'd not be at risk and then, aye, then you might indeed speak from the mountain tops. Why not overlook these petty scruples, these split hairs? The ministers here would make much of the prodigal

---

daughter's return, I vouchsafe that; you and your family would have much to gain, I'd see to it."

"Why do you assume I want these mountain tops? Have you come to make an offer or issue a warning?"

"I come in friendship. To make friendly discourse."

"Then I ask how you could believe that I could overlook the friends who were with me in my home earlier this evening."

"And if not for them?"

"I've wondered. But let me put it to you, sir. If you were given the chance, could you overlook one soul, just one, a small one, in favor, perhaps of certain blessings we were given by God to enjoy, blessings such as love, long life, health, hearth, family, rightful blessings. One soul, could you?"

"One is easier than fifty, or a hundred, or a thousandfold."

"Even if it be your own?"

"Ah! A masterpiece of woman's wit indeed — they say that of you, even your detractors. Among other things. Did you know?"

"More of your misinformation, I take it."

"Not in this case. Mistress Hutchinson: Remember. If you choose, my influence can raise you and your family — or it can undo you. It is only fair to tell you that, after all we are bred from similar branches of old trees. You are not some fishwife to be simply swatted away . . . But I have kept you too long. It shows late, it is time the midwives went home."

"That ruse was your idea, then."

"For your protection. I won't have Bay Colony women treated as witches, I won't have it said we shamed you. Good night, Mistress Hutchinson. My servant will see you home."

A bench scraped back, a pipe bowl knocked against a tankard, footsteps faded away. Light drained from the chamber as the fire was banked. The crack between the floorboards seemed to dwindle till it was only an orange thread in the dark.

I tried the door; it was unbolted. My lantern and cloak lay on the threshold. The house was silent, dim, unstirring. When I reached the bottom of the stairs Anne was gone.

*G*oodwife, I did it . . ."
Through my window came her voice, as in confessionals of old, strained through the shutters' cracks with the ashen light of early morning.

*"Goodwife?"*

"Aye, child, here."

*"Did what you bade, took the draught, Friday week I came, I be the one with that complaint we spoke of . . ."*

Often they come like this, at dawn, twilight, midnight, vague profiles behind the shutters they beg me not to open, dim voices asking for draughts to help start a child, stop a child, hotten a cold husband, warm themselves, cure whatever ill they fear is French pox but seldom is from what they say. They believe I don't know their voices; I let them believe it, 'tis better that way. I never look. An old rule that is, one I have always honored.

*"It goes better with me now except . . ."*

Can't pay, that's likely what, I thought, that's the risk in not looking at them, though next day I might find a bundle of wood or a basket of fish or a yard of cloth by the door, new shoes once, that's the way of it.

*"Goodwife, please a sleeping draught, I can pay, pay now, please."*

---

Her mouth was near, fingers plucking at the shutters.

"Better not, I think. Can you warm some wine in milk?"

*"Nay, nay, a draught, give it to me please, a week not sleeping, can't bear it, I can pay."*

"What is your trouble, child?"

*"Ah Goody Benedict, if only you knew, I thought at first no harm in it but now I see and 'tis too late, can't bear to sit another of her meetings through, knowing what I do."*

"Meetings, whose?" I leaned closer.

*"Hers, hers, Mistress Hutchinson. Surely couldn't do no harm I thought, after all him a minister, no harm telling him what she says."*

"Says when, child, where?"

*"What harm, my husband wants to be churched, this might have weighed in his favor, but near two months gone and now . . ."*

"How long?"

*"May, since May."*

May. When Winthrop got himself elected back in as Governor. But that couldn't have to do with this.

"How often?"

*"After every meeting, but I was forbade to speak a word of this, the draught, please goodwife, the draught."*

"What's this to do with sleeping draughts?"

Beginning to weep, she leaned her head against the shutters.

*"Talking, heard them talking, God help me if they knew."*

"Who?"

*"God forgive me, I eavesdropped on the two of them, heard something I shouldn't, later I thought on it, remembered what happened to Greensmith, dear Lord I didn't mean no harm."*

The weeping thickened her voice, for a moment she couldn't speak.

Greensmith?

Traveling lumberman, knew his face dimly, knew his name only because of his trouble: lately fined and made to repent aloud in all the colony's churches for saying publicly most of the ministers were in a covenant of works, though none but the two who testified against him could recall him speaking so. Scapegoating, some said. Making an example. Mind your tongue now Winthrop's back in power.

*"Back I went, said I couldn't do no more, then the Governor sent for me, the Governor himself, to his house, inside, not just in the doorway, the way it is with the other one. The Governor knew my kinfolk was coming over from England, knew the ship, said with the new Allen Law passed . . ."*

"Go on, child, what else did he say. What about the new law?"

*"He says the magistrates must approve everyone before they be allowed to stay and settle, can it be so?"*

"Aye, more's the pity," I said, "That's the law now." Passed so conveniently by this new court. Convenient for Winthrop.

Conveniently timed with the sailing of a shipful of Anne's friends and relatives from Lincolnshire.

*"The way he spoke I took it to mean my folk would be kept out if I didn't do what he bade, God forgive me, what could I do, the ship was due, dear Lord, the draught please, the draught . . ."*

I thought of Maggie Hett, that perhaps this woman too could be distracted out of her senses, or imagining what wasn't there, or was for some reason of her own breeding rumors, making trouble. But I also knew that I believed this invisible woman, heard in her voice genuine distress, fear, blunt honesty.

*"Beg you believe me, I never meant no harm to a soul, if only I could rest, goodwife . . ."* I wanted mightily to look at her, ask her name, speak with her again. But whether it was owing to the pain in her voice or my own scruples, I managed to crack the shutters and passed a half-dram vial out to her without even looking at the fingers that clasped it.

*"Thank you, bless you, remember, you know me not . . ."*

---

54

She slid a coin and a wampum piece under the shutters so quick they shot across the sill to the floor.

*"Someone's coming watching maybe listening Godamercy I never said nothing."*

I heard her running off. I listened; heard the birds and the gulls and a hound's yap, heard a breeze twitching round a corner of the house and through the garden. When at last I pulled back the shutters and opened the door I saw the medicinal vial overturned where she had dropped it, the stopper dislodged and a half-dram of perfectly good valerian, skullcap, hops, and catnip oozing into the crannies of the doorstone.

Nothing, no one more.

Not till later.

Not till that afternoon, when the Indians came.

Will Dinely saw them first. He had been up on my roof helping mend the thatch when he hallooed for me to come up the ladder.

We watched them move across Boston Neck single-file and silent, forty maybe fifty Pequots stringing out along the narrow spit of land, treading steadily on to higher ground, moving toward William Colburn's rye field; edging it; passing it; turning up the nearest lane to the Common.

We could see their long black hair. We could see their bare backs and the deerskins swinging from their waists. We could see the scarlet sash of the lieutenants and guards, we could see the thick loops of rope binding them loosely one to another by the waist.

We could not, however, see the naked breasts of these Pequot squaws, which is why, I suspect, Dinely wanted to come down off my roof and go have a look.

"I'm close as I want, thank you."

"You're afraid of *captives? Squaws?*"

"Indians."

"Harmless."

"Never."

"Nonsense."

I climbed down the ladder; Dinely leaped from the low slope of my roof in a shower of thatch, shaking the house. A big man, Will Dinely, the barber-surgeon here, and a near friend. Good-humored, talkative, he has a rolling laugh and a doughy belly and several blood-stained aprons he sometimes forgets to take off. He reminds me of the baker at home; always has, no matter how often I've seen him open veins, cut hair, yank teeth.

"You look to have been in a war yourself," I said, eyeing his apron.

"Not this one, thank God. 'Winthrop's War,'" Dinely snorted. "Trumped-up piece of business if I ever saw one."

"Winthrop's vanity," I said. "Wants to be Sir Francis Drake, he does, a war hero."

"Pity he had to send the lads all the way to Connecticut to find him the war, isn't it?" said Dinely. "Our lads go off to fight for a colony we've never seen, against a tribe of savages that's finally decided to let us alone, annoy the Dutch and lose two men while we're about it — small sacrifice — just so Winthrop might hear a hip-hip-hoorah from Boston."

"Ever since he got back in as Governor he's wanted that," I said. "Why else did he go sweeping through Ipswich and Salem? To be cheered. They fancy him up that way, think he's a lord, an earl; God knows they voted him in. Them and those proxy votes he tampered with, him and Dudley, everyone says that election smells, everyone in here knows it. No wonder he had to go to Ipswich for his hurrahs, it shan't be soon that he'll hear them in this town."

"Boston was right not to muster for this," said Dinely. "Sun and moon, atop it all, sending Pastor Wilson as chaplain on a forced march. Insulting, that — after all our pleas for a new Pastor. Winthrop's War, Winthrop's Pastor . . ." Dinely's face brightened. "At least we've Winthrop's squaws to gawk at, come along then, Nell. Let's have a look at them before they're auctioned off or whatever's to be done with them."

"Distributed. Given out as maidservants. To live in people's houses with them, God help us."

"Don't you want one, Nell?"

"Hell's fire, nay."

"Give you a hand in the kitchen?"

"Sounds as if you'd like one giving *you* a hand."

"Nell, you shock me. All the best families are getting one, the Wilsons, the Cottons, the Calacotts, the Stoughtons, at least one Winthrop, at least one Dudley . . ."

Best families and otherwise, everyone had turned out for this half-day holiday: making Boston Common look like one of our old village fairs at home.

The broad grasslands ran on and on beneath it all, supporting that crush of folk, that Indian show, palming it aloft above the tides, the balding field, treeless and open, blending into the marshes and the Back Bay.

The steep whistling voice of a fife spun a tune out over the plain while two drummers rattled out a beat for the training bands marching in formation. Kegs of ale, hauled dripping from the spring, were stacked in a triangle, and leaned against them, with a mug of brew in each hand and a froth on his lips and a large crimson *D* strung round his neck by court order, stood Robert Coles, the brewer's brother and Boston's drunkard, toasting everyone, anyone, and one for the Pequot squaws. The Indians, enclosed by ropes and crates, stood close together, alert, unmoving, like a family of deer staring out at us as if we were the strange ones, now and then making small motions with their hands; roped together at the wrists as they were, one motion caused a ripple up and down the line so that they seemed to be moving as one.

All that afternoon people streamed past them to the marching bands, to the ale kegs and round again. Children raced to reach the pond and back; horseshoes clanged against a post; dandelion fluff blew past my cheek; and all about me skirts swirled russet, saffron, apple-green; jostling, clustering, waving, scattering, what a flurry of folk there was on the Common that day, shifting about like bright leaves blowing across a meadow.

All on account of those frightful squaws.

All on account of Governor Winthrop.

Elegant John Winthrop. A whippet of a man.

There he stood, reviewing the training bands as if they were conquering legions and not a collection of farmers and blacksmiths and shoemakers trying hard to march in step. There he was, former squire of Groton Manor, Cambridge scholar, London barrister, a founding member of the Massachusetts Bay Company, and our first Governor, emerging from his four-year eclipse of power with a reserved nod, a thin smile. A man of the lesser gentry, two generations away from shopkeepers, burdened by ruinous debts in England: here, an aristocrat, landowner, magistrate, Governor. A man who wept for his wife's pain in childbirth both times I saw his Margaret through hard birthings, wept at her bedside and in his library, amidst books on fleshly lust, witchcraft, alchemy, theology. A pious man, grimly religious, judging from the psalms and prayers he chooses as an elder in the church; a man of brittle nature, stiff, sober, never able to draw the affection our last Governor, Harry Vane, did; a man not averse to ruling as a monarch with a tight band of magistrates, a man not moved to trust the colonists with the charter; a man not quite insulted at the epithet "King Winthrop," a man not embarrassed by comparisons with Moses. A man not quite comfortable with bluff red-faced old-soldier Thomas Dudley, now his Deputy Governor; they stood uneasily shoulder to shoulder, black silk to brown serge.

Winthrop moved on to the Indian pen, waving to the crowds in that way he had, making a small circular motion with his hand just above his shoulder. Dinely had by then pulled me along to the enclosure, as close as we could get, quite against my will.

"Some of them are quite young, look at that, she's got tattoos."

"Dinely, put your eyes back in your head."

"Shall they wear English clothes as maidservants . . . or . . . as they are?"

"You're hoping they'll run naked about town? I doubt it."

"Ah, His Majesty is going to choose one. Nay, two. Look."

Winthrop was stepping forward to select a pair of squaws, explaining to the constable that one would need to go by ferry to his married daughter in Newtowne, the other to his niece in Watertown. The Indian women were led to one side and Winthrop joined his hands with theirs, as he offered a prayer over them.

"It is meet and just that you shall now become Christians and it is the Lord's design for this land that it be converted from darkness. 'Why do the heathen rage? I have set my kind upon the holy hill of Zion. The uttermost parts of the earth for thy possession I give thee. Thou shalt . . .'"

I spun round sudden feeling that I'd been stung. That voice. Not Winthrop's, another voice running under his. Female and throaty. Her voice: the one that came through the shutters to me that morning. She was wearing a plum-colored bodice and a threadbare apron and her fingers were twisting the strings as she stood talking with another woman. I did not see her face. I saw her back stiffen, saw her hands smoothing her skirt and stays and cap before she slipped away. Someone was waiting for her on the edge of the Common, the edge of the crowd, someone I could not see at once because the sun was in my eyes. I shaded my brow with my hand and squinted after the plum-colored bodice, growing smaller as it moved away, like a kite pulled in by its master. I walked off a little way, looking from another angle. The sun was no longer in my eyes. I could see the man who had made her shoulders constrict with fear. Waiting on the edge of the Common was John Cotton.

I stood there for a while not moving. The ominous puzzle was completed. I had to tell Anne.


It wasn't difficult to be drawn into the easy, saucy, unrestrained air that hung about the Hutchinsons' house. There was an appealing disarray about the place: the apple-core marking the place in an open book on the table, the overflow of capes and cloaks and caps in the entry, the gleam of marbles and painted tops in the corners of the great hall which made walking there something of a hazard. There was so much talk and clatter and laughter, so many guests and children and far too many cats — nine that year — that this wealthy, privileged home, this social center, was unable, even for a moment, to seem formidable.

And so it wasn't very difficult, even on that alarming afternoon, for me to put aside my errand and let the topsy-turvy-all's-well mood of Anne's house envelop me. I stood for a moment, unnoticed in the doorway, comforted by the simple smells of cornbread baking and the orderly knock-knock of wooden trenchers being counted out for supper.

The big lads, Rich and Francis, were turning the table from the work side, nicked and scarred from twenty years of chopping and slicing, to the company side, polished smoother but nicked as well from all those mugs and plates and children and guests. Once the table was turned and laid with plate by the older girls, the room was transformed: dignified, welcoming, gracious; napkin rings of pewter at each place, the table laid for the family, flowers at the guests' place, and two guests.

"More nutmeg," said Anne, leaning over a wooden spoon at the hearth, where she was supervising supper.

Will Hutchinson, sleeves rolled up, came himself to bang the spice for the custard I smelled simmering, and all at once the household noticed me. The young ones pulled me this way and that, I was drawn into the room, sidestepping the tops and wooden animals that made the Hutchinson floor a hazardous place to walk on the best of days. It was often difficult to speak with Anne alone, but she must have seen the alarm in my eyes and drew me off to the garden. Will also saw the alarm, but mistook it.

"Can't a day go by without someone whelping in Boston?" he said, finishing off the spice. "Let Jane Hawkins tend to it, Nan, and Nell, let you stay to supper. We shall have all your favorite guests this evening and if there is a woman in labor, let Goody Hawkins see to her. Tonight I shall labor, I shall be host and servant. Nan shan't rise from the table once, we'll all be merry; come Nell, why not."

The three of us took a turn round the back of the lot where the kitchen garden is.

"What is it then?" said Anne.

"Informers," I said, drawing a long breath. "In the meetings."

No one spoke for a while.

"I suspected as much," said Will at last. "Reporting? What Nan says?"

I nodded.

"The law requires two witnesses to hail someone into court, seems they've not been able to accomplish whatever it is they want."

"Thank God," I said.

"How long?" said Anne.

"The one I know of, two months. There may have been others before that one though, I doubt this is a new game."

"Winthrop?"

"Partly."

"How do you mean?"

"He doesn't send the informers."

"What then?"

"I gather at some point he hears what they say."

"But he's not the one collecting information?"

"He may be as well. He seems to . . . encourage them to continue." I took another breath. "There's a minister directly in it."

"Ah," said Anne. "Wilson has panicked."

"Not Wilson."

"Who then?"

"Forgive me, John Cotton."

"Nell, that's impossible."

"Why? You speak him fair at the meetings, you repeat his teachings, perhaps he wants to know what . . ."

"Nell!" Anne cut me off. "If he wanted to know what I say he'd ask me, how can you think such a thing of John Cotton? We've known him for years, he sustained me when Zanna died, and Bess a month later gone, he saw me through the loss of daughters, mother, father-in-law, we saw him through his own grief when his first wife died, there are bonds of love and suffering and care between us."

"I know that. But 'twas in a different country, a different time," I burst out. "People change, Anne, be careful. Mr. Cotton needs the other ministers' fellowship, he's not of Roger Williams' mettle."

"You mean that my praise singles him out, puts him in danger."

"I mean he may be frightened enough to do something like this."

"Not John Cotton."

"Why can John Cotton do no wrong?"

"You don't know him, Nell. I'll not hear another word of this."

Anne snipped some rosemary leaves off, threw them in a basket, and went into the house.

"I hope you're wrong," Will said to me. "For all our sakes."

"God knows I hope so too."

"This can't have been easy for you," Will whistled under

his breath, his eyes on the gate behind me. "Nor shall this supper be."

I followed his gaze. John and Sarah Cotton were coming up the path. The Hutchinson children ran to greet them through the long slanting evening light, and I was swept inside with everyone else, with the glow of the summer sunset shimmering on the floor, with the chatter and the laughter and the greetings.

But not for long. I begged my leave, was begged to stay; some excuse got me to the threshold, but not before the family had assembled in two rows behind the benches, everyone there, the last one whipping in like a guilty bird.

In the doorway, I turned to say good evening, and saw that they had begun grace. Something held me there: the bowed heads, the smell of new bread and custard, the sun.

"Let us give thanks unto the Lord, for He is good, for His mercy endureth forever," Will began.

"Bless this bounty of the Lord," Anne continued, "and my family and friends who share it, and please, dear God, inspire Will to ship us a new feather mattress from England."

There was a ripple of laughter. Then John Cotton finished the grace.

"O Lord Jesus Christ without whom nothing is sweet nor savory, we beseech Thee to bless our supper, and with Thy blessed presence to cheer our hearts in all our meats and drinks that we may savor and taste of Thy glory. And bless this home and all who dwell herein, Anne and Will Hutchinson, my very dear hosts and friends and all their kin, through our Lord Jesus Christ."

Amidst the *Amens*, I walked thoughtfully into the twilight.

*The powdered skull of a dead man is said by some physicians to be an able cure for fits.*

*A snail, pounded to a pulp with its shell and swallowed, is said by others to ease the cough of consumptives.*

*Spit, preferably collected from one who is fasting, may be useful in healing afflictions of the eyes.*

*I* must confess I've no experience at all with these treatments, though that may sound countrified and old-fashioned; what skills I possess lie with herbs and I tend to rely on what I know best. But there it is: this medicinal advice scribbled on a bit of paper and tucked between the pages of my *Herbal*. For a moment I cannot think why it is there. Paper that once held needles, perhaps, pricked through in frail even rows. Handwriting recognizable. Placed — as a marker? — opposite a tonic for restlessness.

And then I remember. Where it came from and when I folded it into the book. I remember reading it to Anne. It made us smile toward the end of last summer when smiles were growing scarce, or forced, and a heat spell was unlifting, and breathing was strained, and the bad times had begun.

Thinking back, it seems to me those times grew nearly unbearable the day of that hanging at the new gallows by the town gates.

It was to be a double hanging; the crime in both cases was murder; the condemned men were riffraff off the ships, unknown, unmourned. Ordinarily a public event such as this, attendance compulsory, would have been a spellbinding way to pass a muggy afternoon.

But all the while the condemned men, trussed like chickens and held by marshals, stood for the sermon, eyes were wandering. Eyes flickered away from the raw-timbered gallows, eyes strayed from the Governor, the deputy, the brace of constables; all throughout the sermon eyes kept stealing away to Anne. It shouldn't have been that way. I don't know how she bore it as long as she did.

"I stand before you on this solemn occasion," Governor Winthrop began, "in place of our Pastor who is meeting with his brethren ministers in the First Synod of Congregational Churches. In his stead I shall attempt to deliver fitting words as we bear witness to this age-old and awesome occurrence: the hand of justice raised against those who would bring strife and evil into our midst, those who have broken the commandments of the Lord God.

"Let this be a sign to us all, for this day we come together at a time of great strife and divisions in our own towns. And there are certain ones amongst us who have fostered this strife and troubled our peace, who have done so by casting aspersions upon the preachers of this country. The faithful ministers of Christ have dung cast in their faces: these objections put forth by opinionists and dissenters against the true doctrine if it does not suit their new fancies; fancies which are now rampant in the colony. Indeed when our own Pastor rises to preach these opinionists dare to leave the meeting house or to stand and question the sermon. This abhorrent practice of questioning a learned minister after the sermon is spreading like a contagion to other churches in other towns. The virtue of obedience is vanishing from the land due to the contamination of these new and dangerous ideas. Behold the evidence of this in the persons of these two men who have disobeyed the laws of man and God. Once disobedience begins we must concern ourselves with where it may lead and how far it may take us.

"Be warned: it has become common in this country now to distinguish between men as being in a covenant of grace or in a covenant of works, as in other countries men are distinguished as being Protestant or Papist. Whence can these divisions lead us except to more strife, more disobedience, and the ultimate destruction of our colony from within? Behold the example of the colony of Jamestown in Virginia, riven by divisions, near to perishing. And whence come these divisions?

"From those in our midst who hold with blatant doctrinal errors, blasphemies, even heresies. From those in our midst who hesitate not to circulate and give voice to these abhorrences. From those in our midst who hold with the vilest of misbegotten opinions: that the Holy Spirit and the grace of God may communicate directly with one's soul; that a person may receive immediate assurance from the Spirit, and receive free grace, without clergy or Biblical law as intermediaries, or the evidence of good works as outward evidence to show that one is saved.

"The circulation of these errors can no longer be endured and indeed shall no longer be endured. My brothers and sisters, an assembly of all the ministers and elders of the colony sits in solemn Synod in Newtowne for the purpose of delivering us from this present trouble. The Synod has collected and defined eighty-two of these blasphemies, errors, and heresies, and this Synod shall weed them out of our midst forever. The Synod shall deliver us from these Devil's brats, four score and two, now that they have been held up before the sun that all may stand amazed. The Synod shall deliver us as well from the breeders and nourishers of these distempers amongst us.

"In conclusion, let us now ponder the words of the prophet Amos: *'I will not turn away the punishment for transgressions because they have despised the law of the Lord, and they have not kept his commandments, and their lies caused them to err.'* And let us ponder as well the words of the prophet Isaiah: *'If ye be willing and obedient ye shall eat the good of the land: But if ye refuse and rebel ye shall be devoured with the sword. For the mouth of the Lord has spoken it.'* "

There was a pause.

Anne had remained very still throughout, her face shut and unreadable, chin lifted, eyes intent on some point in the air slightly above and to the left of the gallows, and so she remained as the closing prayer was said over the first prisoner.

". . . Almighty and everlasting God, we beseech Thee to look with divine justice upon this soul in its final moments on earth and upon all of us sinners who truly and sincerely repent."

Governor Winthrop nodded for the drummer to start.

Arthur Perry, the drum on his hip and the sticks poised in his hands and his attention elsewhere, stood motionless.

"Have you anything to say to save your soul?" Constable Hudson asked the prisoner.

"Save my soul, God's blood, save yer own damn souls, who in hell d'ye think ye be, ye narrow canting men, up yer asses with it all."

Winthrop motioned sharply to the drummer.

"Ye turn everything here into a goddamn church ceremony, be Jesus, have it over with, y'ought to be ashamed making a man wait for his death, no more prayers over me, I don't give a fart or a turd for all your prayers."

Winthrop strode to the drummer.

What was said to him I know not; it was brief. Arthur

Perry, as if struck by lightning, suddenly began beating a death-rattle out of his drum the likes of which I never heard and which did indeed accomplish its purpose, almost completely drowning out the remaining words and Winthrop's final pronouncement: *May God have mercy upon your soul.*

The drum rumbled on while they pulled a bag over the prisoner's head and forced him up the ladder to the gibbet; then deeper, stronger rolled the drum as the hangmen mounted the block, prayed forgiveness, noosed the prisoner, and with one long unwinding lunge, pitched him off the ladder. For a moment the rope streamed out loose and languid as a hair ribbon; then snapped taut. The drum roll ceased.

Prayers over the second prisoner began.

Again eyes started wavering to the place where Anne was standing but Anne was no longer there. I had seen her go while all eyes were pinioned to the gibbet, seen her slipping away swiftly, quietly, alone.

Deacon Coggeshall smoothed open a page in his Bible.

I turned, edged off past the fringes of the crowd, and started back to town along the Highway to the Common. The bramble weeds were out, clawing at my hem, and as the road steepened to higher ground a hot wind snatched at my shawl. Below I could glimpse the dark sea spreading round about me like some vast and inescapable stain.

It wasn't long before I saw Anne's skirts flaring out ahead of me in the road. She was walking fast, each hand gripping an elbow, her cap torn off and left to rail down her back by its strings. Through that warm and close day in early September she shouldered her way as if through a freezing February rain.

When I caught up with her she pressed my hand, slowed her pace, but went on glaring down at the dusty ridges of earth under our feet.

We did not speak. We said nothing of the sermon, the Synod, the new sentence for heresy: banishment or death. We dared not put any of these things into words, no matter how much the hanging made us think of them; we spoke of no recent happenings at all.

What we did was walk back to Anne's house and, with that skill for submerging distress in boiling water which we both possess, prepared the midday dinner we were to take together.

We stewed the rabbit. We stirred the cornmeal. We laid the table. We waited with radishes in our hands for the empty town to fill again, and when it did, and the family was gathered into the house, we sat at table. All the while our thoughts were skidding round corners and rushing up steps we ladled meat, wiped chins, sliced bread.

There were perhaps twenty people at dinner, twenty sisters and brothers and aunts and cousins and uncles and infants and friends. And the room was completely quiet. There was no sound but the *knock knock* of wooden trenchers passing from hand to hand down the table and steam hissing out of a pudding and the clank of spoons against kettles; twenty people, bound together by an aroma of stewed meat and baking cornmeal and that terrible silence.

Anne was not eating.

Faith, the daughter who looked like her, the eldest, the bride in the family, was not eating, nor was her new husband, Tom Savage, nor was her gentle-eyed next-in-age sister Bridget.

Will was gulping stew with the manner of a man performing some desperate and demanding act while the younger children gazed from face to face for some sign of reassurance, some explanation for the heaviness of the air in the room.

"Good of you to have us to table today of all times," I said at last. "It must be wearing on all of you, having to go on just as always while the Synod meets, people talk, stare. How much longer can it last, it's run above a fortnight, hasn't it?"

"Ah, they'll draw it out a week more at least," Anne said.

"They delight in this sport, relish it, I'm certain. As if they've found some outbreak of spiritual pox amongst us and cannot wait to come running with leeches for the purging."

"Have they no better wisdom than to gather like gypsies and gabble like hens, reciting these errors they believe they've found in our midst?" Will pushed his plate away. "And has Winthrop no better restraint than to turn a sermon over two dying men into a political harangue, twisting the truth wherever convenient? Shameful, that was, utterly shabby."

"They say the dispute over grace and works is dividing the town but I see otherwise," said Ned, the eldest son, sitting with his wife Kate. "Neighbor set against neighbor by the Synod is what I see, each accusing the other of these absurd 'errors.' At least the ministers have named no names, thank God for that."

"Perhaps they won't." Anne moved an onion from one side of her plate to the other. "I trust we've Mr. Cotton to thank for that much moderation. But the ministers know and I know and most of the town knows that some of those eighty-two 'errors' are in fact my own opinions. My words. My beliefs. Not so many as they might wish, not so many as they've twisted about into gibberish, but there they are, nonetheless. Some. Enough."

There was a pause.

"Enough?" said Bridget into the silence. "Enough for what? What will they do?"

"Nothing," said Will, quick, too quick. "Nothing, chick, they'll do nothing."

"All those people staring at Mother," Bridget said, her voice grown smaller. "All those eyes on you, Mother, as if no one else was there."

"Not only at Mother," said Faith, her green gaze arrowing down the table at Anne. "All of us. Are we all to be made a spectacle of from now on?"

"There, you see, Bridget," said Anne, her smile thin. "I wasn't the only one making a spectacle of myself after all."

Tom Savage looked at Anne through the steam rising from his spoon. "It is difficult for me to understand why you simply refuse to take this matter seriously."

"I know that's difficult for you, Tom."

One of the younger children giggled.

"Mother, this is difficult for us all." Faith's voice was stinging. "Look at how things stand: our Uncle Wheelwright condemned by the court for sedition over a sermon he preached. No matter how long they put off the sentencing how can you ignore that example? The petition on his behalf was rejected by the court, even though so many signed it. All your friends out of power, the only Governor amenable to us back in England, Winthrop reigning like a king with that warhorse Dudley at his side for deputy, and now the Synod. Mother, people know what your beliefs are. Surely they would still know what you believe if you were to keep silent for a time."

Anne set her spoon down very carefully next to her knife.

"Is that what you would have me do, Faith?"

"Yes. Tom and I both, we've stayed up night after night speaking of it. Let you hold back the meetings for a time till winter has come and gone at the least."

"That is what you would have me do," Anne repeated. She folded her napkin into a precise square. "And what of the people who come to the meetings, who draw comfort from them? You would have me tell them that because the times have grown hard we cannot gather here and I cannot speak to them. Because . . . the Synod is meeting? Because . . . Winthrop is Governor? Because my brother-in-law is condemned by the court? Because of these things I can no longer speak what I believe? Tell me, Faith, what would you have me say to Maggie Hett? Shall I say it was only a slip of the tongue when I said God's love surely surpasses our understanding, pardon me, I was tactless to say God does not hate you, cannot be wroth with you if you love Him, shall I tell her to go back to fearing a God of wrath, go back to madness? What of Maggie? What of all those who need our meetings to fill the lacks left by the church?"

"What of us, Mother?" Faith held her gaze level, taut, blistering. "We are your family, not Maggie. Tom and I are your daughter and son-in-law, kin, not just people who sit in this room once a week. We are just starting our lives here in Boston, what of us? How can we hope to prosper here, raise our children here, in a town where the church and the government are turned against us?"

"What sort of town will you be raising your children in if the government continues on this path, barring dissent, frightening and punishing dissenters as they themselves were punished in England? What sort of church will you bring your children to, if the ministers continue on this path, placing works above grace, Divine wrath over Divine love, legalism over comfort?"

I could see the lines in Anne's face as she talked, and I could smell something starting to burn at the hearth.

"Grace, works." Faith whisked crumbs off the table into her hand. "All this over a minute theological point no one will ever remember, let alone understand, in five years — a hundred years — if they understand it now."

"And you sound as if you are one of those who does not understand, else you would see what broader matters this point stands for, else you would see what protesting it means, not only to you, or to me, but to us all, and to those who come after us."

"Oh so lofty as that, is it, Mother? So far-reaching, so visionary, this squabble. I say that is arrogance and I say you would make your own family suffer for your own pride."

"Silence, Faith." Will Hutchinson rose from his place at the head of the table. "Silence. You shall not speak to your mother that way, you shall not speak that way at all to anyone in my house. Tom, get you and your wife home, take her out of my house before I forget she is indeed a wife now and not simply my daughter in need of a whipping."

Faith and Tom rose, crossed the room without looking at anyone, reaching the door with a series of sharp steps that seemed to bite the floor.

"Now look how things stand," Faith said. "Our family is divided as the church and over what? Not a thing, not a happening, an event, an act — over one small belief."

The door slammed.

In the silence Anne, with a tight-lipped smile and a shaky hand, lifted her cup to Will.

"Well," she said, her voice wry, light, "which of us was the one who decided to name her Faith?"

Will managed a tight-lipped smile in return. "Ah, Nan," he said. "The same one who decided to permit her to wed a man named Savage, I should think."

I remember little else about that meal, that afternoon. I only recall scraping all those untouched plates. And the silence in the house. The heat. The smell of burnt bread forgotten in the ashes of the hearth.


The night before the Synod ended Anne and I sat in her kitchen, the two of us alone, the house asleep. It was late; I had stopped to look in on her after supper and stayed. She had seemed to want that. I, for my part, lacked the will to get up and go home.

The heat was unsettling. People had died of sunstroke, travelers rode only after dusk. There was no wind that night but dust hung about us in eerie circles whenever we rose. The candles hissed as gnats veered into the flames, scorching there with an unholy scent. Under my hand the long trestle table felt damp and human. The darkness itself seemed unnatural, even in this familiar low-beamed room: too dense in the corners, too soft, the color of rotting plums. As Anne bent toward the light her face shimmered with sweat.

I held a cool mug of ale against my forehead and watched her press cloves into an apronful of lemons. Whenever I stirred her eyes flickered to my face. Her hands were shaking; a lemon tumbled down her skirt and bumped toward me across the floor. I stopped it with the flat of my palm, oddly distressed by it. A sudden sense of alarm was seeping through my veins.

There was something wrong about those lemons. Anne was doing a November task while the last of summer lingered, making pomander balls to scent lightweight garments that were not yet laid away. Amidst this heat her mind was with winter. I cast an eye round the room once more. The thickening shadows sharpened, took on solid form: heavy clothes heaped in corners, cloaks and hoods and woolen stockings. From the top of the cupboard a thimble gleamed; a mound of buttons spilled over the edge of a pewter plate.

Anne's eyes met mine for an instant.

"Never have liked lemons," she said. "They look like elbows."

Same steady voice as always, slightly husky, the voice of a girl who has caught cold drying her hair.

"Useful, though, that they are," she went on, speaking fast, too fast. "When I was learning Latin I was made to suck on a lemon every time I made a mistake in recitation. Horrid. Truly horrid. The tutor was quite firm about that. I was not a pretty child, Nell. Certainly I looked even less enchanting with my face continually puckered up like a string purse. But learn I did, eventually."

" 'Tis only a rumor, Anne," I said. "And you know that we are all with you."

"Father's idea that was." Anne squinted at a clove she held cautiously, as one holds a rusty nail, between thumb and forefinger. "The Latin, not the lemons. Father filled many hours planning and seeing to our education, even us girls. A silenced minister has a great many hours to fill. My father: I've been thinking of him more often lately than I have in years."

"Anne." I touched her arm. "We've all heard the rumor and we all know what we'll do if the Synod does ban the meetings. We'll stand behind you, everyone who comes here will; why, that's a fair share of the town. At the spring this morning, if you could have only seen the tears, heard the talk, the indignation. Mary Coggeshall said there was a gathering of men in her kitchen last night and there again the talk was strong. Maggie Hett came round this evening before supper with the baby; she'd heard, she bade me give you this. She feared she'd weep if she gave it herself."

It was a sampler Maggie had worked, rows of flowers and her child's name, and her own, and the motto *seek the Light within*. Anne sat looking at it for a long time.

"A week past it seemed simple, what I must do," said Anne, her eyes still on the embroidered cloth. "Simple and plain, while I was still inside that grand red cloud of anger. Anger at the Synod, at Winthrop, and yes, at Faith." She looked up but not at me, at the plate overflowing with buttons. "This morning Sammy came home proper bloodied up, he'd been in a fight. Sammy, the quiet one, the shy one, the one lad that never got into scrapes because he was always off by himself with his thoughts, drawing pictures in the dirt with a stick. But Sammy was in the thick of a fight this time, and that fight was about me, about the meetings. He had dried blood on his eyelashes, Nell. His eyelashes."

I heard myself murmuring those useless assurances: don't blame yourself. Boys will be boys. Everything will come out fine. You mustn't worry. Lads will get into scraps willy-nilly come what may, never mind.

There was a *tick-tick-tick* as a handful of cloves scattered to the floor.

"Steady, Anne," said Anne. "Where is that line, Nell? Where? Where does it become selfishness to stand on principle at all cost? Where is that place, that tiny place, where fidelity to conscience turns into arrogance? How shall I weigh this, having no experience, no sainthood, no extraordinary powers to help me, how?"

"You may not need to make a decision."

"I still need to know the answer."

"Ah. I see."

"Truly? No one else does."

"When that woman came for a sleeping potion and confided in me through the shutters I could not look at her. I wanted to know who she was but I could not betray her anonymity. That is the midwife's morality, perhaps, but what makes me honor it I know not. I only know I could not look. And so I think I know something of what you feel. Something of the agony, only a small fragment, but something."

"Bless you," Anne whispered, and pressed my fingers. "It has begun to frighten me, Nell. It frightens me to think of what may happen if I am made to answer for the meetings, for my beliefs. It frightens me to think of what I may be bringing down on Will, the children, our friends. It never frightened me before but now it does, it crushes me when I think of it, it seems about to bury me. I lie awake at night unable to move, turn over, close my eyes. I think of this room and I see it filled with people, people with whom I feel some bond, some tie, some responsibility . . . I think of this room filled with the children round the table, Ned, grown and with a wife and that wife with child, and the look in Faith's eyes the other day, and Zuriel's eyes staring at me so sober over the rim of his cup, my only New England born babe, Zuriel, and did I wean him too soon because I feared that something might happen to . . ."

"Anne, you'll drive yourself to madness with these thoughts, rest from thinking a while, a little time, tonight."

"Do you know," she said, "I lie awake at night and worry

how shall all the mending be done if I am made to answer for these things. I wonder how shall the winter clothing be sorted out if I am made to answer for these things. I lie there and wonder if anyone else has a key to the sea chest upstairs and why all the gloves I find are left hands and if I'll have time to match them. I lie there thinking of gloves and thread. I lie there thinking of lemons."

We sat there in the hot dim kitchen, silent for a while.

And I told Anne all would be well; of course, she said, somehow or other it would be.

But her hands were still shaking and my sense of alarm had not been calmed, so I took my *Herbal* from my basket and unfolded the note that had accompanied my latest shipment from Perkins, the London apothecary I deal with, who sometimes feels bound to enlighten me on the progress of physick in the Christian world.

I unfolded the note and read to Anne of powdered skulls, and of snails, and of spit.

We speculated upon who might be supplying Perkins; in what quantities; how packed. We laughed a little, the sort of thin laughter that can, for a moment, ward off the dark.

"I wish we were back on the hill," said Anne.

I wished so too.


That day, that last day we had gone together up the hill, we had gone to gather piss-in-beds, we were climbing Windmill Slope and on the slope was plaintain and purslane and burdock — and piss-in-beds, what we call dandelions for the purging decoction they make.

The sun looked like a peach, the skies swept clean, and up and up we climbed, skirts hitched high, singing some old tune in our tinny voices, weeds trailing like streamers from our baskets.

We topped the hill, the hill was ours, and what a wind there was that day, what an angel of a wind.

"I'll be hanged!" Anne shouted, her skirts blown entirely up over her head, where they stayed, billowing out like sails. The sound of laughter from within those yards and yards of snapping cloth was, however, unmistakable.

"I'll see the Governor now," Anne called, muffled. "Show him in."

Tall Anne laughing inside her blue skirts, a breeze straight from England clapping her thin boyish flanks, laughing still as she set herself to rights again, ruffled and flushed and freckled from the sun, her hair in a braid coming down her shoulder.

How many times we spent so, roving about for curative weeds, walking together and telling our hearts, rambling, laughing, there on the hill.


My thoughts came back to where we were, to the lateness of the hour, the mosquito on my wrist.

Anne said she wished she could sleep, if only she could sleep; I was restless as well, and so, we decided to brew up a soothing draught. Anne started water heating over the hearth while I scanned my *Herbal* for something untried, something with chamomile, something with mint. The tasks of measuring and stirring, the chink of ladle against pot were comfortable, familiar. Peaceably silent, we gazed at the scattering of herbs afloat in the kettle but when I glanced up at Anne I saw that she was frowning, and that there were tears in her eyes.

"Foolishness," she said, sharp. "Foolishness, pay no mind."

She turned away and paced about, angered at herself for that moment of fright and prescience or plain weariness, then returned to the hearth and stood with her back to me, wiping her face, smoothing her hair. But she didn't turn round, unable to stop the tears that shamed her so, tears I had never seen before. She said nothing, only reached out a hand behind her back, palm open and upturned, fingers spread.

I took her hand. We stood there for a long time by the hearth while the brew in the kettle steeped itself black.

At my age one doesn't expect to find many new friends, not much above neighbors to chatter with at market, at church, at the door. Certainly this late in life I did not think to find a friendship such as this: the kind that goes deep. Deep enough to make me blind to certain signs, warnings, preferring to wish danger away, to keep it waiting at the back door; not quite real, not yet acknowledged. But one can only do that for so long.

Standing there with Anne I wondered when I had first known and when she had first known that a night like this would be inevitable.

*I* think she saw what she must do that night in the kitchen.

I think she saw what she must do and then pushed it off to a corner for a little time, glancing up at it now and then while she damped the fire and filled the inkwell and braided her hair, watching it during the deep reaches of the night, blinking at it in the morning sunlight amidst the buttering of bread, the baby's bath, through another noontide and another twilight and eventide when the next meeting was to be held.

As I walked through the dark town to that meeting I stopped to watch the moon rise. I stopped to let a cat slink across my path. To buckle my shoe. To tinker with the lantern. To see if I'd forgotten something; anything. How I dreaded that meeting, the empty places, the few voices, the deserted great hall. The danger would keep most people away this night particularly, while the Synod sat in its final hours. The whispers that it would, before it ended, ban the Hutchinson meetings, had become so widespread Boston hissed with them. No word had yet come by ferry across the river from Newtowne, where the ministers were concluding their three weeks of debate. But the ferry landing was lit. The ferrymaster was waiting. This was a night of vigil for us all.

This was also the regular night for a meeting, and Anne was holding one, perhaps for the last time.

When I turned into the High Street I saw another lantern glimmering toward me: Mary Dyer. Thank God. Loyal Mary. Her presence would make that evening easier to bear. We walked up the road arm in arm, slowly, slowly; I told myself that was because Mary was with child. Anne's house winked at us bravely, the torch flaring from the corner sconce, every single window aglow. All that wasted tallow: I thought it, Mary muttered. We did not comment on the front window of the Winthrops' house across the way though we had both seen the silhouetted figure there, unmoving, unhidden, stark, like a tree.

It was Anne's custom to leave her door unlatched so that anyone could enter or leave as they pleased on these nights, and so we did not knock, just let ourselves into the entry. There were no cloaks on the row of pegs — but then it wasn't yet the season for cloaks. The house was unearthly still. My eyes met Mary's but we spoke no word; the stillness had fallen over us like a spell. And then, two steps into the entry we saw why. Two steps into the entry and we could see the great hall: on every bench, every stool, every space of floor, hearth, windowsills, the table, in the corners, lining the walls, shoulders touching, there were people, more people than I had ever seen there before, all heads bowed in silent prayer.

Anne sat on a bench alongside others, a bench set up against the hearth, crowded nearly within it, under the row of twenty-odd candles dipping and dancing on the mantel: the only movement in the room. Her head was bowed as well, but she lifted her eyes when we came in. I shall never forget the look of thanks she gave us from across the room.

Tears stung my eyes.

We found a place, or a place was found for us, I don't remember, and we were drawn into the stillness. I cannot say how long we stayed so, or how many people rose to speak quietly their thoughts as the spirit moved them. I cannot say because time has always spun out differently there in the meetings, long strands of time, full and golden, spun from a new reel.

There is an old woman in Ipswich who came out of England blind and deaf and yet her son could make her understand anything and know anyone's name by her sense of feeling. So it was with Anne's meetings. That is the only way I can explain what we knew, all of us together, there in that room on those nights: there we knew the sweetest sense of peace, deep, and blue as a mountain lake, bluer still, fathoms and fathoms, on and on and on.

The door scraped open; thudded shut. Will was there.

He stood in the doorway and looked at Anne, the spray from the ferry still spangling his sleeve. He stood in the doorway and looked at Anne and she understood.

She rose, looking especially tall amongst all those seated figures, she stood up before her hearth and pressed her knuckles together and began to speak.

"As you all know the Synod has been discussing these meetings even as we hold them." she said, her voice thin but clear. "The Synod has at last made a ruling. Against them. They have been named disorderly and without Scriptural rule, and therefore they are banned."

Anne's hands moved over the table. She gathered up her notes, folded them, stacked them. She put them inside her psalm book. She closed the psalm book, she closed the Bible, and laid them side by side. With the candle-snuffer in her hand she turned her back to us and faced the mantel, slowly, deliberately. Her gown, plum-colored, caught a glow from the fire and firelight caught the gleam of the snuffer in her hand. She began putting out the candles very carefully, very precisely, one and then another and then another and one more and then she stopped.

She stopped and just stood there, her back turned, the gleaming rod in her raised hand. She did not speak; none of us could speak. The purple of her gown seemed to hover round her like a spirit; her spine, so straight, was like a seam running down her back. She appeared not to breathe even when a touch of breeze stirred the dark hair at the nape of her neck.

Then her voice, still clear, almost steady, came out to us though she neither moved nor turned round.

"I will, however, continue to read from Scripture, and explicate the Sabbath sermon on this night, at this time, in the company of my family and whoever chooses to join me. I must caution you all: to meet here is no longer lawful assembly and is likely subject to fine and other punishment. I know there are families and children to consider, to protect. And so. I shall be a few minutes here fixing the wicks I seem to have mangled and setting the candles to rights and I hope that during that time you will move about, get some air, and if you cannot return that is well understood. I thank you all for coming tonight."

With her back to us still she lowered her arm, laid the snuffer aside, and, taking a long taper in her hand, she relit the candles she had put out. All the while she never turned round, giving everyone a chance to leave without being watched.

I closed my eyes, not wanting to see who went out. I heard an infant begin to whimper; a soft hum of voices rising like wisps of smoke, benches creaking, the soft rustle of skirts.

When I opened my eyes again Anne was setting down the last candlestick. At last she turned round but didn't glance out at us. She took her notes in her hand, opened her psalm book, found her place.

At last she looked up.

No one had moved.

$N$ot a hospitable season, that autumn.

A month and a week before Anne was summoned to appear before the General Court of Massachusetts Bay a torrential rainstorm pelted the town and flooded several houses and washed away a new litter of kittens with their eyes still closed.

A day after the summons was slapped on Anne's door, Mary Dyer was brought to bed early with a stillborn and malformed babe, and, knowing how the talk would run to monsters and portents, we concealed the child while Anne sought, and received, John Cotton's permission to bury it secretly without registry, which we did.

A seven-night before the General Court convened a fearful tempest of snow and wind wailed through the lanes, tossed the ships in the harbor, slammed into our houses and spat down chimneys onto quivering hearthfires. The cold panting through every crack, every window, snow hilling up against our doors.

A six-night before the court convened a young man crossing the river from Newtowne to Boston was found frozen dead in his skiff with a half-crown piece in his mouth.

A four-night before the court convened the master of a sizable bark drowned off Natascott while searching for his hat in the icy waters.

*November take flail: let no ships sail,* Grandam always warned.

The snow lay half a yard deep across the ground and chunks of ice heaped up along the river's edge as we crossed by ferry from Boston to Newtowne that morning of November the seventh, the day Anne had been summoned to appear before the General Court.

Creaking at every socket and seam, canvas slapping, the large scow plowed across the water with oars and sails. Spray blew in our faces. Salt stung our eyes. No one spoke. I held onto the combing and stared at the ferrymaster's breath hanging in a cloud before his face. Beside me I could feel Anne, drawn up taut, her arms crossed down in front of her and four-year-old Susanna, the child's face owling out, big-eyed and solemn, from the folds of Anne's cloak. The other young children were with Will to portside, watching the choppy water; the older ones were already in Newtowne with their uncle where they had passed the night with friends, and sat through the morning session, setting aside benches for the large Hutchinson clan. Mary Dyer, not long out of her sad childbed, had gone ahead as well with her husband and children to sit with the Hutchinsons and make notes as needed.

We would arrive in time for the afternoon session, when Anne was expected to be called. Best to be called then, Will said, after everyone has filled their bellies and pipes, taken their ale, warmed their hides, and emptied their bladders.

No one smiled.

The morning session had gone badly, according to Tom Marshall, the ferrymaster: Anne's brother-in-law John Wheelwright, Mt. Wollaston's pastor, banished for sedition; Willy Aspinwall, who had drawn up a petition in Wheelwright's behalf, banished as well; John Coggeshall, deacon of Boston Church, our friend, Anne's back-door neighbor, disfranchised and fined, though they could lay no more to his charge than a difference of opinion. He'd almost been banished, the ferrymaster said, he'd asked if any one among them could cite an example from Scripture where a man had been banished for his judgment, and Winthrop said that if he had kept his judgment to himself and not troubled the public peace with it, he would have been left to himself.

John Coggeshall is a quiet man, his opinions were spoken in private.

If that was the way of it they'd try to make short work of Anne.

The scow plunged on. We began to make out a dark mass along the shore: people, masses of people, come to stare, to catch a glimpse of her between ferry and meeting house, to say they saw her before she went in, to say how she looked, to say she looked brave or brazen or haggard or scared, people who knew her and knew her not, the curious, the concerned, the cranks, the indifferent, the fanatic, the followers of anyone's march; from all over the colony they had come, they were there.

Teeth, a lot of teeth, that's what I remember next, after we'd climbed up the landing ladder to Water Street and the crowd closed around us. Bared teeth, tongues, breath like smoke, people too close, talking, shouting, wishing her well, wishing her ill, wishing she'd stop to speak, wishing she'd go to hell, raggedy men shouting out odds they'd reckoned up for wagers on the trail. We kept a kind of march pace, swift, stiff, kick the hem of your skirt *and* step *and* step *and* keep moving, don't look round, step *and* step *and* eyes straight ahead, walk *and* shake the hand off your arm, walk *and* don't listen, pretend not to hear, walk, walk, walk. It got harder to do, like walking in water, like walking on sand, walking through all these people.

I looked at Anne. She was moving forward and ahead of me with a swift smooth chin-out stride, looking so tall, too tall, too easy to notice, too easy a mark; her hood of brilliant green billowing out in the wind like a banner. Past Marsh Lane we went, past Long Street — the meeting house sprang up before us: a raggedy thatched box it is, more like an untidy squared-off nest than anything else and smaller than ours, chosen for the court's seat so the trial would not take place in liberal Hutchinsonian Boston.

At last we were inside, inside this dim damp splinted house of God, colder than outdoors and empty for just a moment, while we found the rest of the family, took our places. I was aware of the place filling behind us: benches scraping back, the clanging of foot-warmers, a deepening hum of voices; there was a smell of damp woolen cloaks and charring wood, of must and mildew and mice, smoke from the glowing foot-warmers rose, bluish, like incense in an old cathedral, drifting past the small high windows up to the webbing of rafters as the sounds of breathing and whispering and shuffling grew larger and larger round about us.

The murmuration heightened as the magistrates filed in to take their places behind the long table at the front. Simon Bradstreet, the court's scribe, set down fresh paper and quills, and until the opening of the session sat turning his inkpot slowly round and round over the candle flame, testing the contents from time to time. There were, I noticed, writing materials as well at the center of the table where Governor Winthrop, the principal judge, would sit. Most of the magistrates were of Winthrop's circle, Winthrop's mind; he'd packed the court, many said, he'd waited till he could muster this number of conservatives before summoning the liberals, and indeed Wheelwright's sentencing had been put off from court to court for seven months. I glanced down the row of men: Simon Bradstreet, Deputy Governor Dudley's son-in-law; Roger Harklenden, in sympathy with Newtowne's minister; Increase Nowell; Israel Stoughton; grim-faced Richard Bellingham, bitter one-time Governor; John Humfry; Captain John Endicott with his dandy's goatee and his glimmering eyes, temperamental, truculent, an open ally of Winthrop's; Thomas Dudley, arch-conservative, gravel-voiced thatched-headed old soldier, united with his rival

Winthrop by this matter. William Coddington and William Colburn, staunch friends of the Hutchinsons and Boston's representatives, were the only ones my eye lingered upon. The ministers' bench looked equally forbidding: from Charlestown, Anne's oldest critic, Zachariah Symmes; from Newtowne, Thomas Shepherd; from Watertown, George Phillips; Boston's Wilson and Cotton; Roxbury's Thomas Weld and John Eliot; Salem's Hugh Peter — all gowned in black, forked Geneva neckbands stiff and glossy with starch.

John Winthrop, escorted by his honor guard, took his seat at the center of the table with some flourish. I saw him cast a look at Anne only once, when he was settled in place. Her eyes were closed, her face shut in prayer, in concentration, gathering her thoughts, and so she did not see the flick of the slate-gray eyes, the slight incline of the head, the faint flush across the long whittled face, meticulously bearded. Winthrop glanced at Dudley, who was paring his nails with a pocketknife, and glanced quickly away, turning to the inkpot and sandcaster before him. The inkpot had been sitting over a small charcoal brazier and was ready; Winthrop dipped his quill once, twice, and scratched for a few moments on the paper before him. At last he laid the quill down.

The hum in the meeting house began to fade into a hush.

Winthrop leaned forward. The gavel cracked down.

I shut my eyes for a moment as Anne was called to stand forward, as I heard the rustle of her skirts, the familiar stride in that strange aisle. I tried to send all my strength out toward her, tried to hold back all my fear. When I opened my eyes again she was standing before the judge's bench as motionless as she had stood before her hearth six weeks before, deciding on the path that led her to this place.

For a moment it did not seem possible that this was actually occurring.

For a moment Anne herself looked unreal, stiff, carved, all of a piece, dark hair joined to dark cloak joined to dark shoes, set against the continuous ridge of the magistrates' mantled shoulders in eerie relief, as if against some bleak and chilly landscape.

Then she shifted slightly inside her cloak, turned her head just enough to show the end of her nose reddening in the cold. Endicott ran his hand across his mouth. Dudley flicked a nail-pairing to the floor. Winthrop looked up. It began.

"Mistress Hutchinson," Winthrop said. "You are called here as one who has troubled the peace of the commonwealth and the churches. You have spoken things very prejudicial to the honor of the churches and the ministers here and you have maintained a meeting in your house that has been condemned as a thing not tolerable in the sight of God nor fitting for one of your sex to hold. We have sent for you so that, if we find you in the wrong, we may reduce you, so that you may become a profitable member of the community. Otherwise, if you remain stubborn in your course the court may take such action that you trouble us no further."

I could see Mary Dyer's bright hair bent over her own pen and paper next to me. I could hear her quill, and Bradstreet's quill, and when Anne began to speak, Winthrop's quill.

Anne took a step forward, her hands folded inside her cloak, chin lifted.

"I am called here to answer before you but I hear nothing laid to my charge."

"I have told you the charges and could tell more."

"Might you specify one?"

"You have harbored and held with those that signed the petition presented to the court on behalf of your brother-in-law Wheelwright, this morning convicted and sentenced for sedition."

"That is a matter of conscience, sir."

"You must keep your conscience or it must be kept for you." Winthrop slowly leaned forward. "In holding with transgressors of the law you share their guilt."

"What law have they transgressed?"

"The Fifth Commandment." Winthrop paused, his eye flashing to Bradstreet's quill. "The Fifth Commandment has been transgressed here, the commandment that compels us to honor our father and our mother, which includes all the fathers of the commonwealth. Anyone guilty of sedition has dishonored the fathers of the commonwealth and all in authority."

"I am to obey you only in the Lord, sir," Anne said, her voice firm. "And parents who fail to honor the Lord as wisely as their children may be disobeyed with impunity, I think, might they not?"

A ripple of laughter, a shift in the air of the meeting house. Winthrop flushed, his voice rising slightly.

"We do not mean to discourse with those of your sex. You do hold with those who signed the petition and so you do dishonor us."

"I acknowledge no such thing," Anne said steadily. "Nor do I think I ever put any dishonor upon you."

There was a pause. Winthrop's quill dipped, clawed at the paper.

When he looked up again his expression had changed, grown wary, crafty, challenged; I'd forgotten for the moment he had been a lawyer at the Inns of Court in London. He took another approach, in another tone, leaning back behind tented fingers.

"Why do you hold meetings at your house every week upon a set day?"

"Such meetings were being held before I ever came to Boston, and were tolerated then. I see no reason why they shouldn't continue."

"There were private meetings of some neighbors but none so public and frequent as yours, yours are of another nature. Answer what authority from Scripture you have to hold them."

"There is a clear Scriptural rule in Titus, that the elder women should instruct the younger," said Anne.

There was a murmur of approval in the meeting house. Will and Ned Hutchinson exchanged pleased glances; Dudley and Endicott buzzed together on the bench.

Winthrop leaned back a fraction more.

"How does that rule apply," he said, "when you teach not only younger women, but elder women also, and men as well, and not privately but publicly?"

Another stir.

Anne walked the length of the bench, forcing Winthrop to crane his neck to look at her.

"Such a rule applies this way. I am amongst the elder portion of the women of this community, rather than the younger portion, but elder of course does not mean eldest. Elder and younger can also be meant spiritually as well as chronologically. The elders of the church have always taught the others."

"She sounds like a blasted Jesuit," I heard Dudley mutter.

"This is irrelevant," Winthrop called out. "Strike it from the record."

". . . And the meetings to which you refer," Anne continued, raising her voice to be heard, "were private meetings, held in the confines of my own home, and those who came were not solicited."

"You take it upon yourself to teach women," Winthrop snapped, "and yet you do not teach them what the Apostle commands, to keep at home."

"That is misconstrued," Anne snapped back. "You think it isn't lawful for me to teach women, then why do you call me here to teach the court?"

A wave of wordless sound flowed from the back of the meeting house to the front, a spattering of hand-claps, a cheer. I could feel people leaning forward as one.

The gavel banged; the magistrates huddled.

---

Winthrop remained impassive, still leaning back, allowing the noise to run its course.

"You must show more, Mistress Hutchinson," he said, his voice calm, ironic. "You must show another rule from Scripture to justify your meetings."

Anne turned to walk the length of the bench again, coming toward us. Her eyes were alert, almost amused, fixed on Winthrop, as she slowly paced.

"Priscilla, with her husband, instructed Apollo. The people of Berea were commended for examining St. Paul's doctrine. Phoebe was a deaconess of the early church, Deborah was a judge . . ."

"Priscilla, with her husband," Winthrop cut in, sharp, "instructed one man privately: therefore Mistress Hutchinson without her husband may teach sixty or eighty?"

I thought of the silhouette in the window across the street.

"I call no specific number," Anne said. "If they come while I am instructing my family, they may listen, in private, in my own home, where my husband is with me, as Priscilla's husband was with her."

"The witness is not answering the question, strike that from the record," Winthrop called.

"I protest, sir." Anne said. "Show that I do protest."

"Stricken," said Bradstreet.

"You have not shown us sufficient rule from Scripture to justify the holding of your meetings," Winthrop ruled.

Anne looked him straight. "I have given you several apt places in Scripture."

"And none will suit your purpose."

"None will suit yours."

"Impertinent, immaterial, out of order, strike it."

"I protest, sir."

A pause.

"Stricken," came Bradstreet's bland voice.

"Disgraceful." Will Hutchinson muttered. "Even the Star Chamber won't stoop to such low tricks."

---

Again we heard that sickening sound of quill through paper, like nails against glass. Mary wrote furiously on her knee as murmurs rose in the chamber and the gavel cracked again. Anne stood very still, watching Winthrop, her hands clasped under her chin, forefingers at her lips. As the murmuration began to die out she walked toward the center of the table.

"Show me a rule in Scripture *against* the holding of these meetings," she said, "and I will yield the point."

Winthrop stared at her, clearly unprepared for that. His eyes seemed to deepen in color, turning stony. Dudley glared at them both and shifted about on his buttocks.

"She's got him," Mary hissed.

"Your course is not to be suffered." Winthrop's voice came out rough for the first time. "You have seduced honest people from their work and families. All these present troubles have arisen from those who have attended your meetings. We see no rule of God for this, we see no authority for other exercises set up besides the existing ones. If you will not stop these meetings we shall have to restrain you."

"If you have a rule against them from the word of God you may," Anne said, steady.

"*We* are your judges," said Winthrop, an edge to his voice. "Not you ours. We must and shall compel you to it."

There was a long silence. The magistrates huddled together, this time conferring with the ministers as well, while a chair was brought for Anne. At last the men reassembled behind the tables. The questioning was turned over to Deputy Governor Dudley.

"I would go a little higher with Mistress Hutchinson," Dudley began. "Three years ago we were all at peace. Mistress Hutchinson, from the time you came you have made a disturbance and now you have a potent party in the country. Worst of all, you have disparaged the ministers, saying they preach nothing but a covenant of works except for Mr. Cotton and Mr. Wheelwright, who, you say, preach a covenant of grace. This issue seems to us to be the foundation for all these troubles and disturbances. We must take away the foundation and the building will fall."

"You are referring to that meeting to which I was summoned with a friend, and questioned by the ministers, are you not?" Anne began to pace again. I thought of those men as they were that night, when I was perched above them, listening, watching the tops of their heads. Anne went on. "But I never said they preached only a covenant of works, I said some preached a covenant of grace more clearly than others, that was all."

"But when the ministers preach a covenant of works," Dudley said, conspicuously reading from someone else's notes, "do they preach a way of salavation?"

"I did not come here to answer questions of that sort," Anne said, suddenly still, watchful. They were edging nearer to theological questions which could be taken as heresy.

"Mistress Hutchinson, it is evident, knows when to speak and when to hold her tongue," Winthrop remarked.

"That meeting should not be called into question." Anne said. "It was a private gathering, and is protected by the laws of privacy."

"Out of order, strike it from the record."

"I protest, sir, I protest these rulings. 'Tis not right for the court to act as judge and prosecutor both, the one confirming the other's objections and eradications."

"Contempt, strike it from the record."

"I protest."

"Strike it."

"This is absurd."

"Strike."

Hugh Peter strode from the ministers' bench to Dudley. There was another whispered conference, and then for two hours Peter and Dudley tried to prove that Anne had disparaged the ministers by saying they preached only a covenant of works, while she argued against them. The sun and whatever warmth there had been drained from the room. There was a slow spreading of crimson light across the floor; I saw people moving their feet away from it as it began to touch them, without giving any sign that they noticed what they were doing, as if something tangible were seeping across the room. The wrangling over what was said at the ministers' interrogation went on.

"I was there," I whispered to Will. "You know that, I could be a witness. They're all lying."

"You were *not* there, not as far as they are concerned," Will answered, low. "At the time they thought only of the midwife ruse, not that you would ever be a witness. Most of them didn't even know you were up there and would be enraged to discover their brother ministers allowed it. 'Tis better for Nan's sake that you don't testify, Nell; if we keep their tricky secret perhaps they'll go easier on her. If we shame some of them before others they're sure to take it out on Nan in the end."

"Are you certain?"

"Yes."

"But, it might help."

"Even if it did in the short term, we can't have you on the stand, Nell. They might question you about Mary's baby and then Cotton would be involved and it would undo everything quickly. The best we can do is keep them away from a witchcraft charge."

"Dear God."

"They'd have tried it before if she'd been anyone else."

"I suppose, how can you be so calm?"

"If you were inside my left temple you wouldn't say that."

"I wish I could testify."

"I wish you could as well."

"Damn." I noticed I was weeping.

The light was almost gone. The day was almost gone. The first day of the first trial: when I look back at it now those two days blend like screens passing in front of each other, a passage of the same faces, the same words over and over, sliding by very like the oiled paper we use in our windows when we cannot get glass, or afford it, blurring the light of one day into another, without making anything clear.

These fragments remain, repeated over and over in my mind that night and other nights:

"Is this then the charge laid against me, sir, a disagreement in private with the ministers?"

". . . Traducing the ministers, Mistress Hutchinson. Traducing."

"If Mr. Wilson could produce his notes of that conference . . ."

"I no longer have any record . . ."

I wish I could have testified then, that afternoon.

And the next morning.

"I have studied my notes of the conference with the ministers and found things not to be as alleged," Anne said. "The ministers come in their own behalf here to court. Now the Lord has said an oath is the end of all controversy, and I desire that the ministers testify under oath."

A thrum of noise through the meeting house.

"What sign of respect has she for the ministers' words?" Endicott burst out. "You would have ministers swear? *I* do not question their truthfulness."

"An oath is an end of all strife," said Anne, steadily.

"The ministers are so well known to us that we need not take an oath of them, 'tis an insult."

"I have witnesses to prove what was said as well."

The ministers, conferring round their table, looked up.

"Let her first say what she and her witnesses deny and then we will speak under oath," Reverend Eliot began and was silenced.

"Whatsoever is said," Endicott bellowed. "Whatsoever can be said or will be said we will believe the ministers."

Anne was on her feet.

"I protest this remark, let him disqualify himself if he cannot be an impartial judge."

"Stricken from the record as contemptuous."

"Let her witnesses be summoned," said Dudley.

"Who be they?" Winthrop called.

"Mr. Leverett, Mr. Coggeshall, and our Teacher, Mr. Cotton."

"Will you, Mr. Coggeshall," said Winthrop, "say that Mistress Hutchinson did not say what the ministers profess to have heard?"

"I dare say that she did not say what they lay against her."

"How *dare* you look into the court and say such," Hugh Peter rapped out.

"If you take it upon yourself to forbid me," said Coggeshall, "I shall be silent."

He was excused, flushing, already disfranchised, nearly banished, and now totally abashed.

"Poor Johnny," I whispered to Mary.

"Poor Johnny nothing," Mary spat back. "Coward."

Ruling Elder Leverett was called next.

"Isn't this a shame," Will murmured. "To try and nail everything to a conversation in Cotton's house; can't they do better than that?"

"As I remember it, Mistress Hutchinson said only that the other ministers did not preach a covenant of grace so clearly as Mr. Cotton did," said Leverett.

"I suppose it doesn't matter," Will said dully.

"As I remember it, Mistress Hutchinson compared the ministers to the apostles before they received the witness of the Holy Spirit."

"They'll find something to nail it to, Nan," Will whispered to her back. "We're done. If they're willing to piddle like this we're done."

Winthrop called John Cotton.

---

"I did not think I would be called as a witness," Cotton said, "and so I did not labor to recall every word of that conference."

I looked at his sweet face, his aureole of white hair, and tried to see there some semblance of a kindly God-the-Father, but all I could see was that terrible day on the Common instead.

"Did you not remember, brother Cotton, that she said we were not sealed with the spirit of grace and therefore could not preach a covenant of grace?"

There was a silence that went on so long I could feel my neck tightening. I looked at Anne. She was standing very straight, her eyes on John Cotton.

"I do not remember such a thing," said Cotton.

He was very white, drawn; an eyelid twitched.

"Mr. Cotton, your brother ministers affirm it," Dudley blustered, "They stated that Mistress Hutchinson said they were not able ministers of the New Testament."

Another silence. Cotton's knuckles looked like bones. The veins in his head were standing out, throbbing. Anne, watching him, turned abruptly and moved away.

"Mr. Cotton," Dudley pressed. "She said some had not the seal of the Spirit, and that she could know the Spirit's presence directly. Do you stand with us and your brother ministers or nay? Do you say she did not speak this?"

There was another long silence.

I could hear Anne's skirts whipping the floorboards as she paced back and forth in the small recess where the chalices were stored. I could not see her face, only her bent head. Everyone else's eyes were on Cotton.

"I do not remember her speaking that," Cotton murmured at last.

"Mr. Cotton!" Dudley's voice rose. "You do not yet satisfy me . . ."

"Nor shall you be," Anne's voice cut across Dudley's.

"You'll not be satisfied till this court has what it convened for."

Amidst the hum arising from the crowd Anne stepped forward, her mouth tight and grim, hands gripping elbows inside her cloak.

"If you please give me leave," she said, "I shall give you the ground of what I know to be true in this matter. I see how things stand, gentlemen. I see my words stricken from the record. I see a private conference made public, and publicly twisted. I see a friend interrogated almost to the breaking point. Shall I wait while you call up other friends, neighbors, members of my family, and tear them down before this community's eyes? You think to bring me down that way, and in so doing you would bring down those I cherish along with me — and on my account. I shan't let that happen.

"Little good it would do, besides.

"Gentlemen, you did not call me here to acquit me. This trial is a mistrial, as Mr. Winthrop must know. Even by the unjust standards of the Archbishop's Star Chamber, judge and prosecutor may not be one person . . . even there where justice miscarries every day, now. I never thought to see you gentlemen adopt the very tactics that were used against you in England, tactics which indeed drove you from it. Now the persecuted become the persecutors."

She raised an eyebrow, half-smiled; the silence in the meeting house seemed to throb. I felt an inward sinking as I saw what she was beginning to do.

"Even if I got myself off this time, gentlemen, you'd not let me be; in fact you've not let me be for a year's time or longer. Even if I outwitted you somehow, you'd be watching my house, my friends, my family. If one neighbor stepped across my threshold for the evening, that would be branded as a sedition meeting and you'd hail me into court again. There would be other questions, accusations, charges; other witnesses. You'll not be satisfied till you see me gone, that's plain as can be.

"And so, I choose to make a statement now.

"When I was in old England, I was troubled about the churches and the faith, as we all were, and thought at first to turn Separatist, till I heard John Cotton preach, and then did see the Puritan way. This was a terrible wrench for me, leaving my father's church, the church he, as one of its ordained ministers, had struggled with but never turned from. In the course of this difficult time my spiritual adviser, Mr. Cotton, fell ill. I had none to open the Scripture for me but the Lord, as I searched to find a new meaning for everything in my life, especially after the sudden death of a beloved daughter. It was at this time that I realized that one could have a personal experience of the Spirit and that Divine comfort could come directly to one's soul. It was so with me." Her eyes scanned ministers and magistrates, calculating, as she walked by them with her boy's stride, hands clasped behind her back. "And ever since, I bless the Lord for he has let me distinguish between which was the clear ministry and which was not, which is the Beloved Voice and which is not. Now if you do condemn me for speaking what in my conscience I know to be truth I must commit myself to the Lord."

"How did you know it was the Spirit?"

"How did Abraham know it was God who bid him offer up his son?"

"By an immediate voice," said Dudley. "And for you, how?"

"By the immediacy of Spirit to soul."

"How! By immediate revelation!"

"By the voice of the Holy Spirit to the soul. Gentlemen, let us be reasonable. The crux of it all is this: I am expressing what you consider to be a heterodoxy or an error or whatever you choose to name it, and we all know that. I am owning my belief that without any intermediary or outward evidence or works, one can experience the presence of God. One's soul can commune with the Divine Presence. Call that a revelation if you will. It is one of my beliefs. I have many beliefs. I believe, for example, that night follows day. And that vinegar removes bloodstains. I have never actually seen that infinitesimal moment when the following or the removal occurs, but I experience it, and have faith. I publicly own this belief in direct spiritual presence, what you would call revelation. This is my belief, it may not be laid to Mr. Cotton's charge, or to anyone else's." She scanned the row of ministers, her eyes taking the measure of each face. "Yes, gentlemen, this is my belief — and my experience. Yes, I have experienced this direct communion between Spirit and my soul. When I feared emigrating, as my husband wished, I turned to my Bible on a day set aside for seclusion, for pondering. And there were discovered to me passages of comfort: my eyes would see my teachers again, that though I would taste the bread of adversity and the waters of affliction, like Daniel in the lions' den I would be delivered from harm. So I still believe, so I do." Her voice steady and even, she walked to the ministers' bench and stood before it. "Take care what you do to me, gentlemen. If you continue in this course of persecutions you cannot help but bring down a curse upon yourself and generations to come. And I cannot prevent you, but we can all just as well go home and feed our children and light our fires. I spoke to you of the passage from Daniel, what more is there to say?"

"Daniel was delivered by a miracle," Winthrop interposed swiftly. "Do you think to be delivered likewise?"

"Ah sir, you seek to find a heresy even now? I am not that weary yet. No, I expect to be delivered by God's Providence rather than by a miracle."

"What!" roared Dudley. "Where's the difference, where's the heresy, miracle or Providence? Mr. Cotton, now you untangle this for us, if you can."

"The answer is plain," said Cotton. "If she looks for deliverance by Providence I cannot see anything wrong with that. Miracles are what we consider fantastical, possibly suspect, outside the confines of the Word of God."

"Thank you, you satisfy me, sir," Endicott said.

"Nay, nay, Mr. Cotton wearies me and he satisfies me not," said Dudley. "I never heard of such revelations as these even among the Anabaptists. I am sorry," he added pointedly, "that Mr. Cotton should stand to justify her."

"I can say the same." Hugh Peter quickly backed Dudley. "This runs to enthusiasm."

"Mr. Cotton, how do you answer . . ." Reverend Symmes began.

"Mr. Cotton is not called to answer anything." Winthrop banged the gravel again, clearly angered at this shift. "I remind you that we are not here to deal with Mr. Cotton. We are here to deal with the party standing before us."

William Coddington, Anne's only friend among the magistrates, rose. "I think that you are going to proceed to censure," he said. "And I wish to speak before you do."

"Pray, speak."

"You lay to Mistress Hutchinson's charge her discussion with the elders at Mr. Cotton's house, but I see no clear witness against her. You know, too, it is a rule of the court that no one may be a judge and accuser."

"Her own speeches have been ground enough for us to proceed upon," said Winthrop.

"Do not force things along," Coddington said. "For my part, I see no equity in these proceedings at all. There is no law of God or the country she has broken. Consider what you do."

"Come, come, to censure, to censure," Dudley shouted. "We shall all be sick with fasting."

Stoughton and Coddington insisted on the swearing of the ministers, and at last it was done.

"Now," said Winthrop. "What do you remember of her?"

At once all the ministers were down on her.

"She said we preached naught but a covenant of works."

"She said that we were not able ministers of the New Testament."

"She said we were like the Apostles before the Ascension."

"I think that comparison is very good," Coddington called, out of order.

"Silence!" Winthrop slammed the gavel down. "If it be the mind of this court that Mistress Hutchinson for these things that appear before us is unfit for our society and if it be the mind of the court that she shall be banished out of our liberties and imprisoned till they shall send her away, let them hold up their hands."

One by one the hands went up, save for Coddington, Colburn, and Jennison; hammy hands, thin blue-veined hands, a finger raised here, there a fist.

Winthrop rose. Anne rose.

For a moment they faced each other in silence.

For a moment I heard weeping from the back of the sunny meeting house. Mary Dyer's hand tightened on mine, Will's profile was immobile, his eyes on his wife's spine as Winthrop read out the sentence.

"Mistress Anne Hutchinson, the sentence of the court you hear is that you are banished from out of our jurisdiction as being a woman not fit for our society and are to be imprisoned till the court shall send you away."

# PART II

---

# ANNE HUTCHINSON'S JOURNAL

## November–March 1637–38

### ROXBURY

*Roxbury*
*9 November*
*1637*

*I* was brought here by torchlight, here to this strange room in a house, that is not my house, in a town that is not my town. Every night that I have been here I try to walk home in my dreams.

It is a mile from Roxbury Church to Boston Church. Exactly how many steps is that? Exactly. I must try to work that out. There must be a number. It is a mile of walking that I do in my dreams, and all the time that I am dreaming and walking I am taking slow deliberate steps, slow so as not to tire and have to ask for a cart to take me, for I know that to get on a cart, anyone's cart, would bring me back here to this house, belonging to Joseph Weld, of the Roxbury militia, and brother of the Reverend Thomas Weld, Pastor of Roxbury Church: men who are not my friends. The Pastor's house is next door. His motto is "Know Thine Enemy." I shall be convenient for him.

So I see that I must walk, the mud drying on the hem of my skirt and on my shoes, shoes and hem and mud that I see with a clarity that comes only in certain moments of strong sunlight and certain hours of grace. I walk up the High Street of Roxbury, walking away from Rocky Swamp Lane, walking east, I come to Boston Neck. I always arrive there breathless, for I know, I know even in the mistiest form of this dream, that I have to get there before the sun gets too low, before it is level with my apron pocket, for at sundown they close the town gates. There is a rule in this dream: if I reach the Neck before the gates are shut, I have a chance of reaching my home: only then. So far I have been able to cross the Neck, and then I am walking up the Highway to the Common, the scarred dark earth of the road with tall brown weeds rattling in the wind on either side. The sun can set now, I don't care, but it never does. I see the town beginning, the houses tufting up like brown and yellow toadstools, and because I know I am almost there now, I wander south past Fort Field for a moment to see water; to smell it. I stand there on the rocks with the salt candying on them listening to the sea, feeling the air touch my skin, and I feel strong and unweary and unhurried, although I know there is something I must do, someplace I must go; someplace I am expected. I turn toward the town, but it is no longer there. As soon as that knowledge plucks at me I wake.

I wake bolt upright in this room where they brought me by torchlight, and told me not how long I would be here. The court is in recess till Wednesday next, four days from now; perhaps then I shall know. They say they have brought me here because the jail isn't properly finished, they say it is no place for a woman. I say: the jail's back lot adjoins my back lot. It is too close to my own house for the liking of Winthrop and Wilson and the court. It is too close to our neighbors, our friends. It is, to put it most simply of all, in Boston.

This is what was said to me by the marshal who brought me up the steep stairs to this room:

*Here the contagion ends.*

I am thought to be contagious, then.

One isolates the contagious.

I stood in this room while the marshal ran his hand over the walls, trying the boards to see if any was loose; while he tried the window to make sure it was joisted properly, and it had been, with iron nails, not wooden pegs, rare expensive iron nails, and two spikes with heads the size of shillings only moments before had been hammered into the sill and sash to keep the window fastened shut; while he looked about and made sounds in his throat and ordered the birch twig broom removed at once for fear, presumably, that I might use it as a weapon or pry up the boards and perhaps let some of the contagion out if I could not open a space large enough for myself.

*Here the contagion ends.*

The marshal pressed each shiny new nail fastening the window and glanced out again through the greenish-tinted panes of the window. I did not look. I could tell by his face the torches were still there. It was candle-lighting time when he brought me in, just beginning to dim outside. People bearing torches had followed the guard-boat that fetched me here, people in skiffs and dinghies; so many people, so many torches. I could see the lights from the boat, and then from the cart, and when I stepped into this room for the first time I could see their glow through the window.

I did not know then who was carrying the lights. The crowd seemed about a hundred strong as near as I could make out, and the thought of being followed so preoccupied me on the journey to the Welds' that it took my mind from anything larger. I did not know if they had gathered to stare or to shout or to hurl things, I did not know how much ill might be wished me, and I did not want to show the marshal that I feared them. He feared them, and he showed it, and in the boat his sweat had smelled strong as the brine.

Standing here in the room that was to be my jail, watching that glow at the window, I felt a kind of fear such as I have never known. It would have been better had the crowd made some sound, but there was only silence out there. Silence and torchlights. After the marshal went out, and shot the bolt on the other side of my door, I stood for some time in the center of the floor unable to move. At last I forced myself to the window, forced myself to look out. I saw the faces of those who bore the torches: my family, my friends, my neighbors, people from the meetings, people I scarcely knew. They stood in silence for a moment, heads bowed. Then the constables came and shouted for them to go. Just as silently as they had gathered, they went away — except for Will who was let in a few moments later with some of my things, to find me still standing by the window with tears on my cheeks.

*10 November — early morning*

The fog is beginning to break up. Soon there shall be a glint of sun on the roofs. I am up, I believe, at my customary hour, which is half after five. I rise, dress, splash in the basin, and pray for the usual amount of time, as I would do at home. Not because I am pursuing a deliberately planned "prison schedule." Not for any visitors — I am to have none till court reconvenes.

I do this because I have done it for twenty-five years, since I was married at twenty-one. Habit. How else to begin the day, I wouldn't know. A good thing it is that I weaned Zuriel when I did. Another habit that is strong, the next thing I would do: unlace my bodice and suckle the babe. Whichever babe it was.

Habit indeed. I caught myself yesterday morning, without thinking I began to unlace — that would have been a rude shock for the skittish lad coming up with breakfast, pot, and rag, to find me sitting here absent-mindedly baring a breast. Little would he know that I can only dimly recall a time when "the bosom" had for me that rosy shimmer of love and lovemaking: of cool tender evenings and lace and pale, pale powder, of charming with a touch of rosewater here . . . and here . . . of bridal nights, teasing, leaning over, leaning down, of musk and sweet sheets strewn with rosemary.

Dimly I recall that time. It seems to have happened to another Anne. That Anne lived in a body smooth as glass and this Anne lives in a body made almost entirely of bread dough. As for "the bosom," for me it only conjures up the sharp lye smell from diapers and that insistent tug, the smell of sour milk on a fresh linen gown scorching hot from the iron, ah well.

The room is small and plain, about as large as our third-best. An angle of the great chimney runs up the far wall, and my mattress, thin, narrow, virginal, is snug against the bricks. I am too long for the mattress, my feet jut out over the edge, and I get them up against the bricks as soon as I lie down.

In the morning my eyes open on dried ears of corn hanging from the rafters, strings of crimson peppers, and bunches of squash. I wake to the licoricelike smell of drying fennel and the sharper scent of nutmeg, all manner of herbs bunched and hanging up like several untidy squirrels' nests. Barrel hoops swing from wooden pegs, next to skeins of yarn, thread, hemp. This prison was — and is — a store-room. How appropriate.

Here I have my quill, pot, sandcaster, beeswax, and books; a barrel for a desk, a crate for a stool. They've not forbidden me the use of these things, any of them, but I intend to keep this journal hidden; what is not forbidden today may be tomorrow. But in the meantime I have plenty of time for writing and reflection, Heaven knows. I'd no idea how much I missed the noise of our household till I came here.

For the first time since I came into womanhood I have nothing to do. No one calls me, no chores are shouldering their way up to me, pushing other things aside before the next demand pushed forward, before something boiled over or began to burn around the edges, before a crash or a howl meant blood and bruises would be thrust under my nose, before cabbage and sheets and greatcoats became the next concern.

Some mocking spirit must have been listening to me all those times I shrieked inside my head — and out loud as well, I'll not deny it — If only I could have *a quarter hour's peace, a half hour's solitude*, before it starts again: who fell, what hurts, who called, how many spoons, she swallowed what, where's my needle, who got lost, in a minute, watch that kettle, fetch the tinker, buy a bushel, mind your mother, don't do that, put it down, hush-a-bye, no you can't, what's the cost, what's the time, lovely darling, I'll box your ears, fetch more beer, ask your father, where's my needle, she swallowed *what?*

There were afternoons when I could almost see myself shattering into bits and flying apart in a thousand thousand splinters of my self — out the window, out the door, up the chimney, imbedded in the wall, splinters of my soul.

Yes, some mocking spirit must have been standing by, watching me all those years, and now he steps forward with a demon's grin.

There, says the spirit. It's all arranged.

Prison.

And he vanishes in a fit of giggles before I can tell him this isn't quite what I had in mind.


*11 November*

> *If there's ice in November that will bear a duck,*
> *There'll be naught after but sludge and muck.*

I recall stitching that on a sampler a hundred years ago when I was a child and misspelling November.

Well, ice there is, that is bearing several chickens in a large melon-shaped puddle by the cart track leading out to Rocky Swamp. The roads are still yellow with fallen leaves in places and the oaks still hold to shreds of brown leaves, but most of the trees are bare now, and the scent of the leaves is everywhere.

Zanna died in the winter and Elizabeth two months after her. Perhaps that is why I dread it so.

It does not please me to recall that this month was called Blot-month by our old Saxon housekeeper. Blotmonth. The month of slaughtering cattle and hogs; month of blood.

I see men passing me below with large aprons over their clothes, the aprons stained brown-red, and the women passing with the hems of their skirts stained brown-red as well from the earth.

Today was, in the old church, Martinmas, a feast day that always fell at slaughter time, and as long as I can remember was held to mark the beginning of winter. Poor St. Martin, what did he do? Halved his cloak, I think, and gave it to a beggar who was the Christ. I believe St. Martin died of exhaustion after attempting to eliminate the death sentence for heretics.

Perhaps I might reconsider him.


## 16 November

Ah this is wicked, wicked.

I knew the court was again in session but had no idea that this was to come:

My brother-in-law Edward Hutchinson and our friend Bill Balston were summoned to court as "opinionists," and both have been disfranchised. In addition they have been fined most cruel hard as well, forty pounds each. Edward turned his back on his judges and told them if they take away his estate they must support his wife and children, and for this he was hustled off to prison overnight.

They have allowed Will to come and tell me — not out of

kindness, I trust, but because they know I'll believe him. My poor husband, running about from his wife in her prison to his brother in his; it would most certainly kill his father, whose greatest joy in this world was that the Hutchinson family made something of itself. Well. Make something of ourselves we have done and I'm glad for old sire Hutchinson he's not walking this green earth to see how it differs from his accounting.

The court has gone on to punish other friends:

Tom Marshall, the ferrymaster, whom I last remember holding a turkey drumstick at my table and leaving small tidy-shaped patches of grease on my cuff when he clasped my hand to bid me good evening.

Willy Dyer: dear Mary's husband, they brought him in as well.

And Rich Gridley who repaired our chimney and sat with the Dyers and the Marshalls and the Balstons and the rest in my house. All were publicly admonished and disfranchised.

I feel a twist of pain, of guilt.

If I'd not held the meetings.

If I'd not persisted in holding them in the face of the ban.

Captain Underhill is to be called to court tomorrow.


*17 November*

Underhill did not give way, would not repent his association with the opinionist faction. Men of the sword may speak freely to their employers, he told the court and added that Joab had spoken roughly to King David.

Underhill has been disfranchised like the others. And worse: dismissed from his office, stripped of his command. A professional soldier he is, had always been, not a Sunday militia man marching in his leather britches and brick-dust axle-greased shirt with the training bands. They took away what he held most dear, and all he knows how to do well.

Ah John.

Today Will does not come, cannot come, must stay at home to sort out his affairs and be with the children; he has been in court and here and back in court again for much of the week. Today it is Nell who comes again and stands under my window throwing pebbles against it while the Weld family is at table for a quarter-hour grace before noon dinner. Clever Nell. They'd none of them dare interrupt the prayers to interfere with her. And there she is, there is Nell standing below in a green mantle and two mufflers wound about her neck, the mufflers coppery in color like her hair, Nell standing like a fragile small rosebush wrapped up in sacking for the winter.

She says rumor has it that I shall be imprisoned only till month's end. Thank God, I say, thank God. That is something to hold onto, ah thank God. Ah, and how, I ask, are the Dyers, the Underhills, Balstons, all the brave folk who stood so firm?

They do fine enough, Nell snaps, and adds, a far better cry than the lot over in Charlestown under the thumb of our dear Reverend Symmes. And then she stops, lips pressed together, like a small child who has in mid-confession suddenly decided not to say another word.

"That Charlestown lot that came to the meetings every week without fail, Mr. Sprague, Mr. Richardson the constable, so loyal, so faithful, so spiritual, Sergeant Edward Mellows, Ralph Mousall . . ."

"What's happened to them?"

*"To* them? Happened *to* them?"

"Nell. What have they done?"

"Threw themselves on the mercy of the court. That's what they've done. Repented their association with us. All most graciously forgiven. Court adjourned with unusual speed as if it was afraid anyone else might get out of being punished that way." Her voice suddenly tired, the sting gone. "Ten of them. Called themselves penitents, acknowledged their error."

There was a silence.

"I'm sorry I told you," Nell said at last.

"Never that, Nell. I want to know. Well. I won't have to lie awake nights over this lot will I?"

"Don't try to cheer me up."

"I'm trying to cheer myself up. Ten families are now to be in trouble because of me."

"Hell's fire, no one's in trouble because of you. They're in trouble because they thought a thought and followed it. They're in trouble because the court decided to make trouble for them. By God, they're in trouble as they choose — or choose not — to be."

Watching Nell go was difficult. After she'd left me I saw I'd held the ragged edge of the windowpane so hard a thin thread like a line of blood was etched into my palm.


*21 November*
*Tuesday*

Winthrop's gone mad, I think.

The court has ordered all the colony's powder and ammunition removed from Boston to Newtown and Charlestown. It claims there is a strong suspicion of Antinomianism that they, as those in Germany — Germany? *Germany?* — "in former times, may, upon some revelation, make some sudden interruption upon those that differ from them in judgment." The court has moreover resolved to disarm all those who signed that petition circulated on behalf of my brother-in-law Wheelwright, when he was condemned by the court. Of course anyone who signed it went to our meetings. It is a tool to punish my friends.

Antinomian. That terrible word. Anti: against; nomen: the name. Against the rules, rigid laws, literalism, legalism.

Against a world based only on works. In favor of a religion emphasizing a state of soul or grace, on the spirit of the Gospels. I thought that was what we believed. But of course it isn't, really, what they mean when they try to label us with that name.

Antinomian: Almost as bad as being called "Witch." Worse, today, really, since no witches have been sighted recently in Massachusetts. Antinomian. A word synonymous with murder, demagogues, false prophets, religious frenzy, and dissension. A fearful word, associated with the religious revolution that almost destroyed the German city of Münster three years ago. I know little enough about that disaster. As I recall, a strange sect led by one John of Leyden which held all in common, property and family alike. With great disorder, they rioted in Münster, ousting the appointed authorities. There followed privation and violence. Is this what Winthrop fears. Is this how he sees me? Mistress Leyden of Massachusetts. I could almost laugh. Am I to believe that Winthrop, and Dudley — or is it Wilson, has it been Wilson all along? — seriously expect Boston to begin a revolution? An armed revolution? Against the local authorities. Over my cause? They see me as an anarchist then? But why should Winthrop see any similarity between Leyden's Münster and our Boston? There's no cause, no reason, no logic behind this, and that means I can no longer begin to guess what can happen. I had hoped the punishment of the few would stave off the punishment of the many and was wrong.

It begins to remind me of what we fled from in England, when people were so afraid, when the Archbishop's spies were everywhere and Puritans were hounded, boycotted, dragged into the Star Chamber for questioning. I remember how John Cotton fled in disguise to the ship that brought him here, pursued by agents. And now an agent of the court marches up the High Street, Will says, knocking on doors.

The constable went with his list up and down the streets and lanes of Boston serving the court order, summoning the head of the family, reading the order aloud, to each. Within ten days the householder must deliver to Mr. Keayne's house all such guns, pistols, swords, powder, shot, and match as they shall be owner of or have in their custody, upon pain of ten pounds for every default. However, if the householder would attend on the court and acknowledge his sin in subscribing to seditious libel he might be exempted from the penalty of this order.

Will said you could hear the knocking on doors up and down the High Street, over and over again you could hear the order read out like a chant.


*23 November*

It hasn't taken long.
Within only three days ten have recanted in Boston.


*24 November*

Five have come forward in Newtowne and denied they ever had anything to do with me or the petition on Wheelwright's behalf, saying their names were added without their consent.


*25 November*

All in all, thirty have recanted in Boston by now out of fifty-eight. William Dinely has gone before Winthrop and confessed "the sinfulness of his course." Dinely, Dinely, sinfulness?

Sam Cole, my neighbor, has acknowledged "the error of his ways."

Tom Oliver, church elder, and young Johnny his son, who just a little time ago was sent to represent Boston at court on my behalf; they have both admitted the misguidance of their thoughts.

Isaac Grosse, the brewer who paid me and Nell in special dark ale when we helped his wife birth twins, Isaac whom Boston Church rejected, Isaac has acknowledged "being led astray." Ah, but I suppose that is to be more expected than from some of the strong ones, the churched ones, the Dinelys and the Coles, who have never been bullied and set apart by church and state.

We know people in so many different ways; we seldom, in a life, know how they would behave in the line of fire or at a deathbed or in a moral choice. The jolly soul you lift your cup to at your neighbor's house, the friend you meet every morning at the spring, every morning for years of your life, you know her, and you know him, but you do not know if they would reach for your hand if the house caught fire or if they'd take your part were your name defiled. You cannot know these things of people, not until they happen. They cannot know these things of themselves, not until they happen, perhaps. I myself did not know with absolute surety if I would use all my wits to defeat the court or if I would make certain I delivered myself to their feet, not until I got half-way through that trial. We cannot know. We do not know. But with good friends, friends that seem to have been born into the world as brother or sister in spirit if not in flesh — with them we think we know. We believe we know.


*26 November*

Tom Wardall and William Wardall. From *Lincoln.* My neighbors from *home,* from *Alford;* our oldest friends here. Acknowledged error. Both.

And I am told this, not by Simon leering in the doorway, nor by the Welds watching me with eyes like small gray faces within faces, nay I am told this by my son-in-law Tommy Savage. Faith could not bring herself to come.

I am told this seated on the writing barrel, having offered Tommy the crate. Company seat. Beyond his head, out the window, I can see a slate-colored sky and sharp bare branches which appear to be rooted in the low clouds, growing from them toward earth in some unnatural and bony arrangement. Outside a puppy keens. Tommy's breath smells of meat; his face, when he brushes mine with it in greeting, is frosty.

He has been in great agony of mind, he says.

I am sorry to know it, I say.

Faith has been in great agony of mind, so great she is keeping her room.

I shall write her again, I say.

"Better not," he says.

There is a long silence. I can recall silences so choked and pulled in tight and hard to breathe in, but not often. I can recall a silence when I was asked to give an answer I didn't know at lessons, and I can recall such a silence when I sat with a suitor whose hand I was about to refuse, and I can recall that silence when I asked the doctor if Zanna would live.

"I have come to see you," Tommy says, "because I am a man of honor."

I say nothing. I remember that many times I can't much like Tommy nor he me, though since he wed Faith, I've found it unnecessary to hold that opinion in my apron, polishing it and turning it round and round; there wasn't time. Or interest, I suppose. My fault.

"I am a man of honor," he says again, a trifle too loud. A creak in the floorboards just beyond the door suggests a quick movement of an ear away from a crack. "A man of honor, of depth, of thought, serious thought."

"Well then, what can be the trouble?" I cannot pretend to myself that I don't hear the sarcasm in my voice. The edge. The edge Faith knew she would hear or she would be in the room with her husband. This daughter I never understood, never could reach, married a lad I cannot understand or reach either.

"I feel I owe you honesty, truth. It is a point of honor. You have tried to be a welcoming mother to me, you have had me at your hearth, at your table, and I believe in your prayers. You have endeavored to be a good mother to me, a hospitable friend; you have given me material gifts and offered me gifts of the spirit, and I know you've been sincere."

"Tommy." Still the edge in my voice, an edge I don't want there, an edge that I cannot seem to keep out. "I thank you. But what's this about?"

"Just like you, Mother." His face changes slightly, or it is a trick of the light? "You think me not serious, lacking depth, incapable of thought."

"Did I say that?"

"You had no need to."

"I'm sorry to have offended you."

"I take no offense, I'm used to the scorn you harbor for anyone in your family you deem lacking."

"That doesn't jump well with your speech of thanksgiving a moment ago."

"You always were able to slice right through the words to the point, weren't you?"

You could put eyes out with a voice like that.

"Ah Tommy, let's stop this, can't we? Tell me why you've come."

I had a strong idea.

"Very well, no cushions and velvet then."

Another pause. I could see the idea looming off to my left, rising against the wall with the door in it, dark and tall, an idea I knew I wasn't going to like at all when I looked at it straighter than from the tail of my eye.

"You knew our feelings before the trial. Before the Synod banned the meetings. Before you held the illegal assemblies. Before, you knew our feelings before."

Looming there against the wall by the door it is no longer

an idea that I see from the tail of my eye, it is certainly broad-shouldered, tall as the room.

"Faith and I have talked about this every night," he goes on. "Often till dawn. It is our joint decision."

He cannot get to the point.

"And so I thought it best, we thought it best, that we be open about this."

I will not help him.

"I've been to see Winthrop. The court. I've confessed the sinfulness of my course and asked my name to be stricken from the petition on behalf of Uncle Wheelwright."

This feels worse, far worse than I had thought it would. Pain, anger rise like dust before my eyes.

He stands up fast and knocks over a small keg which rolls a pace or so. "You cannot expect us to be untrue to our consciences any more than we should expect you to be untrue to yours. Can you?" He paces. "Mother? Can you?"

"Sit down, Tom. Please. Sit you down."

He sits awkwardly, his face unhappy. I take a breath.

"You are right. I cannot keep your conscience for you, cannot expect the dictates of yours to agree with the dictates of mine nor the other way round." I keep my voice even.

"Well. It's all right then. I've been in such agony of mind."

I am weary of trying to be good. Weary, weary.

"It has been so terribly difficult, the torment of deciding."

Weary of trying to be patient.

"It's all right then," he says again.

"I cannot say it's all right. I cannot rejoice over what you and Faith have decided, and if you thought I could at least feel compassion for your struggle, perhaps that is too much to ask. We cannot expect to govern each other's consciences, but we must always expect to affect each other's hearts."

"It took courage."

"Indeed."

"It did. And Mr. Winthrop, Mr. Dudley, they were all more than gracious."

"I expect they were. It must have considerably brightened their spirits, watching a member of my own family come a penitent."

"Loyalty to conscience exceeds loyalty to kin, and you believe that, else you'd have stopped the meetings when there was still time, you'd have thrown yourself on the mercy of the court, by my faith you'd have done something to spare what you've brought down on all of us."

"Have you fetched a hammer and nails?"

"I beg your pardon?"

"Loyalty to conscience above family does not mean cruelty to one's family."

"You think you've not been cruel to us? Oh not in words, not in the way you and I are going at each other now. I mean in what you've done."

"They didn't warn me I'd be granted a new judge and a new trial after less than a fortnight."

"That's always your way, Mother, the quick retort, the jab of wit, and underneath . . ."

"Underneath I feel great pain. Does that surprise you? Please you? Have you got what you came for?"

"I don't know why I came at all," says my son-in-law. He calls for Simon, who flings the door open so fast and with such force he pitches into the room.

Tom, without another word or glance, strides out.

Tears blur the doorway for me.

"My best to Faith," I call after him, my voice sounding dry, scorched.

That night I wake with my back coiled tight and my eyes burning and know that in my dreams I have been crying for my old nurse, for the maple tree that sheltered me in its arms when I was a child.

Another rock through the window.

The third night in a row.

Each night the rocks have come at about the same hour: just after the town snuffs its lights and banks its fires and gets itself to bed. Early enough to avoid the Watch, they're still readying themselves to come on at nine. Late enough so that the lanes are empty. Dark enough so that the head and shoulders of a woman in a rare still-lit upper-story window must seem suspended alone and luminous as a waxen seal against the sky: a good mark.

The night when the first rock crashed in through a windowpane and landed with a small skip and slide in a corner, tearing down a cobweb in its rush, I cowered. I dropped to the floor like one under fire; I lay flat and shaking for perhaps an hour, expecting more rocks, shouts, a rain of rotten fruit, expecting to lose my supper, my nerve, my pen down a floor-crack, half expecting rescue from the Welds, splinters in my palms, glass in my eyes, sudden death. Poooooooor Anne.

None of these things came to pass.

After a while I felt stiff, foolish, my back began to ache, and I got up, doused the candle, went to bed.

Last night, the second night, when came the second rock, I cursed. Oh I did. My anger felt mighty, large enough to fill this large house and split the wallboards open like seams in an old gown.

I cursed as I never in this life have done, never, God forgive me; pounding the sill, I spewed words that would, we were warned in childhood, stain our tongues black forever, I spat blasphemy and bawdy-talk from London's back streets and Alford's barnyards; shouting in a whisper, the whisper due, not to propriety, but to the fear of that powerful wrath within me; if I'd given it more voice — I don't know what. As it was, the child who pointed a sticky finger at me outside the meeting house and screeched *Holy-Annie-Holy-Annie* would have been shocked into silence by the curses which sprang, unstoppable, from my mouth like frogs.

To tell the truth I surprised myself.

I don't even know what all the words mean.

Tonight, the third night, I watched them gather down there, three or four of them, murmuring, dim figures, and when they seemed ready I stood back. Closed my eyes — safety precaution. Did not cower, did not curse. Laughed, for some reason, surprising myself again. A short dry jerk of a laugh, rather like a cough. Is this progress?

The Welds have chosen to ignore this matter of the rocks.

Or so I gather. No one speaks to me directly.

I've an idea they were warned ahead of time, that's the only way I can explain the quiet in this house after each high-pitched tinkling crash. Not the sort of things one sleeps through, not the sort of sound one passes over without comment. The first night I thought I heard a very small involuntary hissed *goddam* on the other side of the wall but cannot be certain. The Welds, I believe, take this burden of housing me, imprisoning me, as an honor. It means they have a bigger house than anyone else, it means they more than anyone else can afford to feed another mouth with ease, it means above all that they are good, so good that my presence will not infect them.

But how wonderful it must be for the lads of Roxbury to throw rocks through the most expensive windows in town, to pelt the house of the richest merchant, to behave like bad boys half their age and know they'll go unpunished. I'm sure of that. This is fair play, I should think; just as it was fair, at home, to throw apple cores at people sitting in the stocks; I did it too.

And so there's nothing to stop it.

I just hope the Welds don't run short of rags to stuff in the windowpane; winter's coming.

Each rock had a note attached, wound round it with string, each with the same message. Each misspelled. Is this why I laughed?

YOU HORE, the first one read.

The second, revised, improved:

YOUR'RE

A HOORE.

I detect a Dutch influence in that spelling. And noted the rhymed couplet.

The third, a bit more ambitious, showing an expanding vocabulary:

YOU HORING HARLIT

Obviously these lads are not reading their Bibles thoroughly. The spelling of these words is set forth quite clearly therein. Ah but the ministers have warned them away from those passages that contain so-called "questionables," and the "questionables" must be the worst words they can think of; they know not what to call me, the charges were so unclear, and although harlotry was of course not in question, they want a wicked word. And finding one, or two — cannot spell them. The lads who wrote these notes are educated, I see by the penmanship, the paper, and just think: they shall enter the new college, the new Cambridge, unable to spell *whore* and *harlot* properly. The first students with such a disability, I'm certain. Imagine what would happen if we grew incapable of spelling all the words that disturb us.

In any event, tonight I was fast.

Tonight I grabbed rock and note, and with my pen already inked, corrected the spelling, bound the whole together again, and tossed it back out the window before the group disbanded below.

Then quick, ducked beneath the sill, shielding my face

from what I knew was surely coming. Cheeky Anne, I hissed to myself, look what you've done now.

And so it was most unexpected when, as I crouched there scolding myself and cringing, I heard laughter in the street below.

Not mocking laughter. Merry. A cheer, *hear, hear.*

And more laughter.

It's been a while since I've heard that sound, full and warm and spicy, like mulled cider cupped by the dark.


*28 November*

No rocks last night.

Perhaps the lads are off trying to find words I shan't know how to spell.

Perhaps the Welds think three holes in the window are enough and let that be known.

Ah well. Persecution in mild doses can become a distraction, especially when the persecutors are on the other side of a stout wall and do not avail themselves of gunpowder. I am, after all, not terribly brave, and am not at all taken with the idea of genuine persecution, prison-fever, punishment of mind or body. Which is why I station myself near the window for most of the day, trying to keep looking outward, not inward, trying not to think too much about why I am here and for how long and what comes next.

If I do not go to the window and look out and watch what happens beyond it I begin to phrase certain questions which not only disturb me, they make me pace, something I do not wish to do because that can be heard easily and for some reason it offends my pride just now to be heard pacing. If I do not go to the window punctually as a prim schoolgirl arrives at her desk, I hear clearly formed questions:

They banished my brother-in-law and Will Aspinwall and gave them a fortnight to leave.

They banished Roger Williams nearly two years ago and gave him the same.

Why then have they banished me and still not said how much time I have in which to gather my possessions and leave? Why let all the others at large until they quit Boston and lock me up in another town?

Can they think that I would be more dangerous at large than my brother-in-law, who has an entire congregation at Mt. Wollaston who might heed him? More dangerous than Aspinwall, writer of petitions, who could summon the same numbers of people to his house that came to mine?

What else do they have in mind? Is this the end or is it not? Are they frightened of me? And if they are shall they treat me the way most people treat those who frighten them? Will there be another snowfall before we can reach Rhode Island, will the weather hold, will Boston hold its temper, will Winthrop and Wilson and the other ministers hold theirs? Will Cotton help soon or is that too dangerous for him?

*What shall happen mama what?*

*Whatever happens dearest we shall be together.*

*Whatever happens it shall be over soon . . .*


*29 November*

Tomorrow is the month's last day, the day Nell heard I'd be set free. 'Tis the day I have not allowed myself to look forward to straight on, but only let myself have short sidewise glances at now and again. No writing on the walls, no reducing the days into sticks and crossing them off with other sticks; I've not done it and won't.

After Captain Weld and his brother the Reverend Thomas Weld appeared at my door, and after they'd stood there a while in silence after it had swung open, I knew. They didn't need to tell me it isn't over yet. I suppose I knew the day they began punishing our friends. Joseph Weld, his face like a slab of raw meat, his breathing thick and greased with gravy, contemplated me.

They both contemplated me for longer than necessary although it was perhaps shorter than it seemed. I was told that I am to remain in custody. Custody. How droll. Avoids referring to his house as a jail, which would certainly bring it — and its owner — down in society. Winthrop says "the richer sort" do not manage jails. "The poorer sort," "the meaner sort" do. Captain Weld is a custodian then. And so he shall remain for some time. I ask him how long.

When the current disturbances are terminated, he says, after a quick exchange of looks with his brother. That could mean soon, I suppose; soon those who stand by their beliefs will be disarmed and those who recant in order to remain armed will have done so, and with the rest banished or planning to leave, it should be over. Then again I do not trust these men and I do not trust their definition of trouble and I do not trust their definition of terminated. I am not even certain Captain Weld knows what that word means, and suspect he was rehearsed by his brother, who went to Cambridge while Joseph was learning commerce. Nell is right. I do not suffer a fool charitably.

"We are gratified to learn," said the Reverend Thomas Weld, "that six have repented here in Roxbury, three in Newbury, two in Ipswich, two more in Charlestown."

I say nothing. I am watching the strings of crimson peppers waft to and fro over the men's heads, caught in some draft.

"Ah yes, and five in Newtowne at least," Captain Weld adds suddenly, with all the fury of a schoolboy who has remembered the answer to the teacher's question after he has already been asked to resume his seat.

Nell did not go far enough.

I not only suffer a fool badly, without charity, I mock them in my mind — but not out loud, not this one — I want something from him. I want to be let out of his custody.

Idiots have custodians, as do the blind. As do estates. As do empty houses.

I want to leave this custodian and I want to see my family. Never mind which order. I ask.

I receive what is nearly the exact same answer, only this time there is an amendment.

When the current disturbance is terminated, *it will be discussed.*

I say nothing. I cannot say, "I see." I don't see. For a moment all is dark and I can see nothing at all. I don't know, in that moment, why I am here, why I have chosen this path, why it is worth this pain. This terror. Within me a frightened child cries out, lost.


*30 November*

Market Day this morning, Lecture Day this afternoon. Everyone is in the Roxbury Meeting House for the afternoon Lecture and the town has that stillness I have come to know since I have been here, for the first time outside the meeting house watching the silence curl over the town like a leaf.

Confrontation in Boston Church last Sunday considered another "disturbance" I wonder?

Our friends were incensed by the proceedings of the court, but the new law of seditious libel has placed Winthrop and his colleagues comfortably beyond the reach of criticism or chastisement by private persons. But they saw that while Winthrop was yet a fellow in the church convenant with them he does not stand above the admonition of the church. Determined to express their resentment several of the congregation consulted with Wilson and Cotton, urging them to admonish Winthrop in the name of the church.

Wilson was by no means disposed to reprimand the Governor for pursuing a course with which he was wholeheartedly in accord. Whatever Cotton's feeling he saw fit to reject the scheme.

Seeing the possibility of greater troubles, one or both of the ministers informed the Governor of the plan that was afoot. Winthrop grasped the meaning of the situation and seized the initiative himself. After the sermon that Sunday he rose from his seat and informed the congregation that the church had no authority to inquire into the justice and proceedings of the court. Both in rule and practice, Christ had disclaimed such power, he reminded them. As a private person, Winthrop conceded, a magistrate was, like any other man, accountable to the church for his private failings, but the church must not presume to call a magistrate to account for his official acts, however unjust they might seem.

For himself, Winthrop insisted, he had always sought to follow the dictates of his judgment and conscience in providing for the public good. He would offer but one ground for his judgment in the present case: "Those brethren were so divided from the rest of the country in their judgment and practice, as it could not stand with the public peace, that they should continue among us. So by the example of Lot in Abraham's family and after Hagar and Ishmael I saw they must be sent away."

And so Winthrop is above admonition.

And I? I suppose to him I am Hagar. A concubine.

Cast out with a bastard brainchild to wander in a desert was Hagar, after Abraham's wife Sarah bore him a legitimate heir.

Hagar, the handmaid to Sarah, the concubine to Abraham; and the unacceptable love-child born to Hagar, her infant Ishmael, was sired by her ruler turned exiler.

Have we, between us, spawned troubles for Boston, Winthrop and I?

Or is it simply that he didn't consider the matter of concubinage to be a part of the story. I am amused in spite of myself. Here endeth the lesson.

## 7 December

During the past week I have felt too ill to write, or read, or do anything but gaze at the window or curl against the warm brick wall of the chimney. At first I thought it was the disappointment that had thrown the four humors of my body out of balance with one another. I disapprove of despair, and even more so of illness purportedly caused by it. And so I have disapproved of myself.

My grandmother regularly got "the lying down disorder" whenever she was in despair: in her case whenever one of her favorite relatives married or moved away or died; in the latter case the family funeral bed carved of rosewood and hung with heavy black curtains would be sent for and placed in the great hall for the lying-out. After the departed's remains had been carried to the churchyard, my grandmother would lie herself down behind the curtains of the black bed in great despair, finding nothing to rise for in the mornings, and nothing to appetize her at mealtimes. Now in the nights I see her again, her old skin lying like long pale feathers against the bones of her face and the eyes staring at the canopy, eyes wet and gleaming.

What ails me? It cannot be disappointment. I remember too well my intolerant young face turned away from my grandmother; I remember my scornful resolve never to be like her.

What ails me? God have mercy upon us, I think I know.

## 8 December

I cannot stop laughing, I cannot.

It shakes my quill, this laughing, and in truth it's not a laughing matter to be with child again in my forty-seventh year for the . . . fifteenth? . . . sixteenth time. It will be hard, the last time was hard as the first time, and yet I laugh.

I have hope again to pass this winter, however cooped up and silenced, amidst my family. Will is concerned about me bearing and birthing here in prison and shall try to have me confined to a room in my own house, if they must insist on incarceration. This sort of thing embarrasses Winthrop, and perhaps he will try to make short shrift of it all and tell me to leave, turn me out in the cold. I wish he would. I'd sooner cross trackless snow with morning queasiness coming on than be moored here to this room, a room that seems to be growing smaller as time goes by.

## *10 December*

Very solemn day.

Day of verification. Authentication.

The verification and authentication of my condition, that is to say whether I am indeed with child or only playing a female trick on the General Court of Assistants of the Massachusetts Bay Colony.

The General Court of Assistants of the Massachusetts Bay Colony is at the moment very much interested in my urine. They do not say so but there has been quite a flurry, consultations with the Roxbury midwife and with Nell and Jane, with Dr. Oliver, with the Pastors of both churches, and this concerns the basic question of how to find out definitively and accurately, and maintain propriety at the same time.

The Roxbury midwife is reluctant — understandably — to involve herself in this, afraid that whatever verdict she presents she will be summarily punished, set in the bilboes, removed from midwifery of Roxbury or the state, or, most importantly, lose her following among the women here. There is some feeling among many women that a midwife can, if she has assisted at the birth-travails of bad women, bring down ill luck on other birthings, and that fear is precisely what is keeping her, as I heard Simon tell it, flat on her back with a mysterious malady that prevents her from turning even on her side.

That presents the authorities with a dilemma. It presents them with Nell and Jane, both known to be skilled in midwifery and the healing arts, both respected by women and men alike for these skills, both frequenters of the Hutchinson house and meetings and worst of all, both my friends.

There is an unusual amount of excitement over this, a stir partly as if I have, in the act of conceiving, done something illegal; partly they fear that there will be sympathy aroused if it is true.

Nell arrives at my door, looking mischief. Simon stands guard, his eyes on the basket she carries as though it may contain an entire set of alchemist's tools or a charm that might turn him into a twelve-pound lobster.

"I should think this is a misdemeanor," Nell says, still standing in the doorway, straight and tiny as if she is perching on the sill, head cocked, birdlike, keen as always.

How it is good to have Nell in this chamber with me. I cannot stop my smiling. We embrace, the tough straw of her basket catching at my linsey-woolsey skirt like worried fingers.

"You be well?" she says, low.

"Ill as I've ever seen."

She holds me at arm's length and frowns, her eyes turned sharp and impersonal, looking at me as she has looked at hundreds of women throughout her life, the midwife observing, noting, checking for certain signs. She whispers, before letting go my arm, that Dr. Oliver shall be coming and almost directly. He has been deputed by the court to observe all that she does; he is known to have repented his association with me and is a ruling elder of the church besides, therefore, considered trustworthy and a mitigating presence next to Nell.

I begin to laugh.

Simon looks alarmed. Nell frowns.

"Anne," she says low, between her teeth. "Not a merry thing, this. You're too old to be breeding again. You've born too many, 'tis dangerous. We'll talk of it later, listen now: he'll come and watch you make water. To verify I've not switched or tampered with nothing."

"Ah dear sun and moon and stars above." I sit on a barrel, shaking with the laughter. "Watch me make water, stars."

Simon gasps. Nell's lips twitched.

I have an abrupt sensation of the cold china of a chamber pot making a half-circle against my bottom, sitting there as a child, waiting and being watched as I waited. I remember the window I gazed up at, its small panes rectangular and even, dividing up the light and the sky beyond into neat safe packages, and I remember the window gazing down at me, and how the warm light felt on my bare shoulders as I sat there, my mother tapping with her fingernail on the chamber pot's lid.

"And then," says Nell, "He will examine the beans I put into the water you make, and he will put half of it in one pot to take with him and another to leave with me and we will add his beans to my pot and my beans to his pot and he will watch to see if they sprout at his house . . ."

"Under guard. They'll get a guard for the urine. A pot marshal." I go on, unable to stop this wonderful fizzing of giggles, grateful that there is something absurd enough to laugh about, that there is anything to laugh about at all. "A blessed constable on urine duty. Good sweet heaven, are they afraid someone will witch it with the chamber-lye of a pregnant woman?"

Nell has dissolved, Simon has bolted to the corridor, and Dr. Oliver enters with Reverend Weld.

I know they do things this way for the royal household. But really, what possible difference can it make to these men if I am bearing, aside from the fact that it might evoke a bit of sympathy? Or is it curiosity? Fear that this will let me out of jail?

But they are here, the ritual is begun.

Not that it's in any way needed: all they have to do is ask me. I've borne fifteen children, I ought to know how it feels to be starting another.

Solemn-faced, bearing a chamber pot before him like a holy offering, treads Dr. Thomas Oliver, my friend before a mere ten days ago. His servant is carrying the kidney beans. Silently pot and beans are passed to the minister, who nods. They look at Nell, whose lips are twitching again. We are trying to look at each other as little as possible.

Nell's pot and beans are examined. Pots and beans are switched so she has his and he hers. I remain standing by the warm chimney wall wondering how they're going to manage the next part. Dr. Oliver is a physician; he deals with illness in the most abstract way. Dinely draws blood, sets leeches, amputates, draws teeth, binds wounds, stitches up the bad ones. Nell has for some time prescribed medicinal cures to the women and children, and presided at childbed with Jane and me assisting, as it is unthinkable for a man, out of modesty's sake, to treat the female complaints or birthings. This leaves Dr. Oliver more of a gentleman farmer, church elder, medical consultant — and just now extremely discomfited.

He coughs and asks if I would kindly take a seat.

I glance at the two shining chamber pots.

Oliver flushes.

"I meant have a chair," he says. No chair in sight. He flushes deeper. Nell's shoulders are shaking. I sit on the large barrel while he looks at my eyes, my tongue, my hands, then straightens up, moves back.

There is a long silence. He and Weld look at me, away from me. They look at Nell, away from Nell. We refuse to offer solutions, we refuse to help them at all, and spin the silence out. Simon's breathing can be heard from the passageway.

At last, however, the midwife in Nell grows impatient with this silliness, this delicacy, and gets on with it.

If they are concerned over the process, she begins.

"The authenticity," Weld corrects her.

She advises that if they are concerned, why do they not stretch a sheet over a corner of the room and place first one pot and then another behind the sheet. That way there can be no question of anyone being alone with Mistress Hutchinson, no question of anything irregular, and shall we begin.

The men seem pleased. They won't have to look, they won't have to watch me squat, and they won't have to leave Nell alone with me.

But they can listen.

And so it is done, and the pots are borne away, one by Oliver, the other in Nell's basket; she is watched at all times by Weld, and will be watched all the way home by Oliver.

Three days later the beans have bloomed, it is undeniable that I am with child, and there is whispering all around me in the house. People stop under the window. Will visits every day. Rumors: I shall be set free, I shall be locked in my own house, and Will is so hopeful, so pleased, so frightened.

I dare not allow myself to think that they might send me home.

The last disappointment was so great I cannot bear to build a staircase to another one. Also Nell has told me that despite Will's hopes, and the people he has talked with, and the efforts he has made, the most reliable talk says this childbreeding will not remove me home. The fear is greater than ever that my condition will touch those who repented their association with me, and that they shall feel ashamed, and feeling ashamed shall make reparations. Winthrop has broken what he calls the faction and he will do nothing to risk its revival. My childbearing state seems to have unduly alarmed the authorities. This was something they hadn't bargained for: life stirring within me, here in this prison, here is this bleak winter. It means to them, I suppose, that in some mysterious way I am not destroyed or even controlled. And, what if I die of it, I'm forty-six, it's not a far-fetched thought. Will they have it on their souls?

I remain ill. There are great pushings in my middle and I am with the chamber pots more often than Oliver or Weld could have wildly dreamed. I vomit and wipe my mouth and lean my back against the brick wall, warming it, warming the seed within. I am tired from feeling ill and so am spared the pain just now of having to think about this month and the next and the next.

But when the queasiness lifts off and the weakness quits me for a few moments I think of this blessing, that even if it is a serious danger, it is a gift, and one that grew in the dark of prison; conceived the night before the trial and carried with me to this place, where it has come to make itself known and felt, like a sign from God that even in back bedrooms and bad times of the soul, there is life, life, life.

*13 December*

The ministers come often now, nearly every other day; they come somberly up the stairs, their tread specific and slow as if they are carrying something heavy, and slowly, specifically, they knock.

They knock.

Why they knock I have no idea as I certainly have no way of letting them in and Simon is always scrabbling up the stairs behind them to unlock the door.

Perhaps they knock to alert me to their presence, or to show that we are all civilized beings, or to make certain I am not astride the chamber pot. Or perhaps it is a sign of their authority, as their knocks are not polite and tentative questionings, these are gavel-like raps. They have come, their knocks make clear, to labor with me.

For the good of my soul.

For my spiritual estate.

For my salvation.

They have come to fight a manly battle with a force so dangerous it must be locked away with the drying fennel and the wizened peppers and the frightened-looking crookneck squashes; they must labor mighty indeed with this breeder of Boston's late distempers, this source of contagion only trusted not to affect vegetables.

The ministers' faces are grayish in the light here, the skin lying carefully arranged against their foreheads and cheeks and chins. Their hands immediately fold neatly, left into right, like wings on a sleeping duck. Ah but their eyes, their eyes are alive, eager as a suitor's, curious as a child's, and lit with the eerie brightness of cats' eyes in the dark.

I know what they are here for.

This is a grand spiritual and theological exercise for them, in the dreary idle days of winter, a chance to talk as they did in seminary, to debate points, to feel that flex and stretch of the mind as it approaches, tilts with, angles on certain questions, new ideas. We talk about theology, we speak of works and grace and which has the greater priority, we discuss resurrection, spirit, soul, matter, we quote Scripture at one another as if we are in a seminarians' contest, we hone the point smaller, smaller, till it can barely be seen at all and can only be felt with the tip of the mind.

I love it. I look forward to their visits. It is the only thing that keeps my mind alive now, these questings into spiritual matters that I have always loved; the shuttlelike rhythm of the debate, and these men have fine minds, fine minds. That I must say. These discussions do more than help pass the time, they keep my own mind alive and fresh, enlivening my wits, and during them, my queasiness retreats, waiting until the session ends.

It is usually Thomas Weld, sometimes Shepard, often Davenport. The men's pleasure escapes me not though they try to mask it, and their excitement, for these are the kinds of discussions that took place many evenings in my father's house, and I knew even then it was hard to sleep after them.

The ministers come for another reason as well: I think they want to fathom what it is I was saying at the meetings that drew all those people, and brought those people something they never found in Wilson's sermons. They want to know what nature of thing this is, this woman, what comes off her tongue. I do not know precisely why all those people came, it cannot simply be that Wilson's sermons were arid and frightful, and scared the children and offered no comfort to us, pilgrims and wayfarers far from home, strangers in a strange land. It cannot be that alone. I wish I knew what it was I had given, for then I could rejoice in that now, and it is a time when I could do with some rejoicing, with some sense of peace and gratitude over a past action. Maybe I shall find out what it was in the course of these discussions.

And so I am grateful for these ministers and their scriptural questions. Never mind that I know they would think it the greatest of glories to them if they could make me recant; never mind that I know this prospect has not entirely escaped their attention, and indeed is one more reason for them to come.

Will is furious, Mary Dyer is upset, brother Hutchinson appalled, and Nell swore like a South End London fishseller when she heard.

"Why do you let them badger you?" they demand.

Ah well, it is hard to explain that these gray men who come and sit like stone urns, unmoving but for their eyes and lips, these men who have come to help save my soul are helping to preserve my sanity.

I saw them coming down the lane, my family, all of it, cloaked and mantled in brown, hooded and solemn-faced, like a company of monks on a journey. They were coming down the lane, Will leading, coming to my window and oh then they were monks no longer, no staring eyes from the High Street kept them stoppered within that crystalline propriety, they broke ranks and the younger ones jumped up and down and skipped, and everyone was waving arms and talking at once, then oh then they were mummers, jugglers, troubadours, come because they alone had invented cheer and knew how to do it. They held up gifts they'd brought, they waved and waved, then paused, heads cocked, heads turning, someone is saying something to them, something I cannot hear, only the voices, two females, flowing like a thin trickle of water, soft and cool from the front door. The heads come up, there is a great deal of pointing and mouthing words I cannot make out because there are tears in my eyes and new glass in the windowpanes.

They vanished, smiling, just as the bolt on the other side of my door was shot to and the door opened, and Captain Weld in a voice like a steer lowing told me I might go down and greet them.

We have no Christmas any longer in our church but this was like the Christmases of my childhood, not the Mass, not the going to church, but the gathering before and the gathering after, the embracing and greeting and everyone talking at once.

The cat climbed up inside the chimney and the Welds retreated; they grew more distant as I listened to each household misdemeanor, each tale, each word, and touched each face. A bit of a present was brought forth one by one: articles of nothing, that put together, would make me a fine homecoming costume: a bonnet; a muffler; mittens; a bodice;

kirtle; petticoat; and never you mind that the muffler was only long enough to wear with a wing extending on each side so as to give the appearance of a woolly green butterfly and never mind that the mittens were slightly different shades of blue and one so large you could play paddle ball with it, and never mind the bonnet with the ribbons uneven and the petticoat made of kersey in a wedge down the back amidst the linsey-woolsey, where the material had run out, I'd happily go in tatters, with my family come to fetch me home.

But I was not to be fetched home that day. I should have guessed from Will's stony face that could not be gladdened by all the merriment.

When we were given a few moments alone in the upstairs room, while I was changing into the costume the children had made, he told me, rattled it off fast, as though he'd memorized it as a lad does just before a dreaded class recital:

Due to the severities of the season:

Due to the frailties of my sex:

Due to the late disturbances in the colony:

The merciful judgment of the court is that I am to be kept in custody by Captain Joseph Weld of Roxbury, confined to one room, causing no further disturbance and having no conversation with any but my immediate family and the clergy, until March when the roads shall be passable and I may depart this jurisdiction forever.


*16 December*

Very bright and clear with a cold wind from the northeast. For a week now the birds are coming to be fed but I have naught to give them. Every morning there is a hard white frost and fog. Winter has begun in earnest and I am downcast. Because it is winter, because I am to be a prisoner so many months. Well, not so many months, three only. A quarter of a year. But today, it seems a vast space of time which I must cross like a sea.

I was prepared for the banishment.

I was not prepared for imprisonment. And now so much of it, such a long span of it, months. Why should prison seem the worst of it? It is the worry for my family. It is the wonder too of what they mean to do with me here. I cannot trust their sudden concern for my welfare and wonder what it is they want from me now. They want something, this I feel. A recantation? Or even more horrid, perhaps they will want to examine me the way small boys do insects, examine me so that they may learn precisely which heretical and seditious opinions they must guard against in the future, and why these same opinions drew such a large following.

Know thine enemy.

Anne, enough.


### 20 December

Will has come to visit with the youngest children, thinking they needed the visit the most. The small bodies so stiff inside my arms, stiff in that way they've always been when sad or scolded.

Bridget waits outside with the carter, comes in for a kiss and an embrace that warmed me through, then shepherds the children out, leaving Will and me alone for a few minutes. We stand facing each other, my two hands in his two hands and we move no closer, as if afraid that if our bodies touch, we shall hunger so the pain of denial will be worse than the pleasure.

The winter is already becoming a hardship in Boston, there is such a great shortage of wood this year, more than ever before, that Will thinks I shall be warmer here in Roxbury. He pauses after he says that, smiles expectantly. He meant that as a light and gently merry idea, almost a joke, and I smile, nod, shake my head, smile again. There must be the usual confusion of boats and skiffs and struggling to get to the island, fell trees there and haul them into our treeless plain of a town. There shall be stools in the hearth of many a cottage soon, Will says. I ask him if he still wonders why I hate winter.

All night long I hear the wind blowing, and below me in the evenings I hear coughs. People pass below the window looking reddened, as if by a sudden force, about the edges, hands, noses, ears. Simon's nose looks chewed and scarlet. The birds sit puffed up looking like elderly ladies bundled up and waiting for the buggies to fetch them to church. I wish I could stand in my front window at home and see the "vessels swaying at their mooring, creaking under the load of ice on bulwarks and rigging." I cannot say my spirits have lifted more than three hands high from the floor, but feel a bit better hearing of Will's plans. He and Coddington, Coggeshall, and brother-in-law Ned Hutchinson, Will Colburn, Sam Wilbore, and others have met together in secret; what I feared the night before the second day of my trial has now become their fear as well: No formal charges have yet been preferred but they are aware that they may be "marked as quarry" and are not certain that what they are calling Winthrop's Ten Days are over. Coddington had received a letter from Winthrop which made clearer the intent of the magistrates to move against him. They want to break, exile, and cow what they call our faction, but I think Winthrop is afraid of Coddington for another reason. Winthrop is a lawyer, was for many years, and knows he conducted a mistrial. There was no jury, but he'd passed a law saying it wasn't necessary, although that is a still questionable point, under English law. But he knows he acted as judge and prosecutor and that even in the Star Chamber, that constitutes a mistrial. Coddington knows this, and is now perhaps the most important and wealthiest man in the colony beyond the other magistrates. He could make trouble over the patent, he could involve his friends at court, and they cannot allow that to happen.

The trials over, he, Coggeshall, and Colburn with some others drafted a fresh remonstrance against the actions of the court saying they saw no equity at all in its proceedings. Winthrop wrote back: "You have broke the bounds of your calling that you did publish such a writing. You go about to overthrow the foundations of our Commonwealth and the peace thereof . . . against the rule of the Apostle who requires every soul to be subject to the higher powers and every Christian a man, to study and be quiet to meddle only in his own business. I earnestly desire you to consider seriously of these things, and if it please the Lord to open your eyes, to see your failings, it will be much joy to me and I doubt that the Court will be very ready to pass them by and accept of your submission."

And so plans were being laid out. Why should not they and some few others remove quietly for their peace and settlement? Boston was not the whole of the western world nor was yet Massachusetts. A rich and pleasant land lay beyond them to the south; near Mr. Williams was ample room for another plantation. Will intends to negotiate the land purchase himself with the Narragansetts but they are keeping this dark until spring when they can travel to the land near Rhode Island and set about this great new plan.

And so my spirits lift somewhat. Will seems happy. He has always attained things so easily, and then once the attainment comes there is a need in him for the conquest of something new. His excitement I think will be contagious to the children, or so I hope.


*24 December*

My grandmother had sayings for everything. Her favorite for this month was *In December keep yourself warm and sleep.* I've heard worse suggestions.

---

There was this morning a sharp frost and thick fog. The fog cleared off about nine in the morning and the sun shone brightly. I longed to take a walk, to go out and feel that cold damp air on my skin. Every twig on every tree and bush was outlined in silver tracery against the sky; some of the dead grasses growing by the roadside were sparkling with frost in the sunshine. I think I saw a flock of birds down on the fields, and a pair of bullfinches in a hawthorne bush. This is a mild spell, and I can see groundsel starting to bloom, and ground ivy. Every mild morning in December, the birds sing from the thatch on the roof across the street; there is no thatch on Captain Weld's house, 'tis modern shingle like my own roof, but the birds across the way appear to be singing to some other birds above my head on the ridgepole and I long to see what they are. This mild day is of course a fluke, and shall not come again, and that makes me want to jump out into it with both feet.

My restlessness is at its greatest point since I have been here, longing to get out and run, run, run with my arms flung open, sending out all the pent-up vapors of my body into the wind. I long to hitch up my skirts and let the world see my woollen stockings and little I'd care if I could gallop down a lane and dance circles on the frozen grass.

### 27 December

But what a gift. Mary Dyer come to me. Walking right in, mistaken for one of my own daughters, with two of the littlest ones she held by each hand, Kitty and Susanna. Mary is a golden girl like Faith, with that hair that fairy changelings have and the long delicate fingers and the strength that remains entirely hidden. She was swathed in mufflers as well, and when Simon let her in and watched us she embraced me with her hand over my mouth at the same time so I wouldn't say her name.

I talked with each daughter while Mary looked about the room. I talked with Susanna, who is four, about how I walk up and down taking as many steps as I think would go between here and Boston, here and her bed, and she has promised to walk with me at candlelighting time. And we shall try to talk to each other, then, I say, and ask her if she can do that: even if it seems no one hears her, I am indeed listening. And the small stiff back loosens its sinews, one by one, as though this poor child is removing an invisible corset, and she looks up at me, studying my face for a while.

"You look different," she says.

"I? How?"

"As if you just rose up from bed."

"You've seen me that way many a time."

"Not in the afternoon." She traces her finger under my eyes and down the sides of my mouth and across my forehead.

"Thank thee, Susanna," I say dryly.

"I expect you're getting old." She sighs and goes off to play with the drying pumpkin rings.

Delightful. Child of my heart, delightful. Soon I shall be frightening them all. Mary unwraps slowly for the room feels so deliciously warm to her after Boston's chill; no house is really warm, she says.

We talk, we talk as the light puddles across the floor and seeps down the cracks between floor and walls, receding like water draining away with the afternoon.

After Nell, Mary is the friend I love best: friend since we met crossing together on the *Griffin*. We were the only women who had the unseemly hardiness, quite calloused and manly, it was said, not to be seasick.

Mary has patience for the sort of spiritual exploration that wakens my wits and makes them lively — the sort of discourse I grew up listening to in my father's house. The sort of discourse that also puts many people directly to sleep, but not Mary. She is quick, keen; talking of doctrinal points and Scriptural exegesis, of Inner Light and Outward Works, our minds mesh. The two of us can sit for hours as if we were two schoolgirls chattering about new gowns. How I have missed our talks during my time here; how good it is to have her here with me again.

We speak of small things: spools of thread; the sharpening of quills; our studies; the Scriptural messages we set ourselves to ponder. We talk the afternoon away with Susanna asleep in my lap.

*30 December*

"Troublemaker," Simon hisses under his beath as Mary leaves with Susanna. He has just realized his mistake. He has been listening at the door too, I have no doubt.

*Troublemaker.*

Of course I'm a troublemaker, I'll not deny it. Too weary.

After supper I huddle with the quilt Will brought me, a quilt from my bed in Alford, from my narrow girlhood bed, a quilt I have often huddled in when I've been unable to sleep; cold, fearful, alone.

It is a bit discouraging to know that at my age I am still reaching for the fleshy comfort of down-filled cloth. A bit disturbing to find I'm longing for some hot milk laced with honey, and in here with me, in here with the quilt, a hot brick wrapped in flannel. Come, Anne. You'll be wanting your mother next. But never mind. Some soothe themselves with rum, some with poppies, some with music, books, sweets; some calm their fears by believing themselves to be Good Queen Bess, others by calling on the devil. Sailors soothe themselves with the sea's motion, and so perhaps it isn't such a shameful thing for a forty-six-year-old woman wrapped round and round in a downy quilt, knees to her chest, back to the warm chimney wall, to rock and think and rock.

This child within me, this seed of a child, who shall they tell you your mother is?

*A troublemaker.*

Aye, well, and so was your grandfather.

You come from a family which refused to learn.

Stubborn, stubborn, there's a streak of that, but more.

Your grandfather was in 1578 called before Saint Paul's Consistory in London, November it was, nearly the same day I was called before the General Court of Massachusetts. Your grandfather, Francis Marbury, was an ordained minister from Northamptonshire, a land far away, where he had already been imprisoned and released for his preaching.

He stood before the Bishop of Peterborough who had ordained him, and before Bishop Aylmer of London who presided over the ecclesiastical court, and before Sir Owen Hopten, and an Archdeacon and other members of the High Commission. Imagine the dark paneling and the bright robes, imagine the light falling through mullioned windows, imagine the holy smell of wood polish and mice and incense and old stone.

Imagine Bishop Aylmer asking: "Francis Marbury: Now you are come, what have you to say to my Lord Peterborough or to me?"

And imagine your grandsire answering back, "I come not to accuse but to defend. I say the Bishops of London are guilty of the death of souls, souls which have perished by ignorance of ministers the Bishops ordained, knowing full well they were ignorant and unqualified."

He was, child, arguing for an educated clergy. He believed, as do I, that the clergy shepherds souls and therefore bears a responsibility for each soul in its charge; and so if they know nothing but rote prayers and have no inner spirituality, no learning, scant knowledge of the Gospel, how could they shepherd a soul any better than a blind man leading others to the fair?

Said my Lord Bishop, in return, "You are speaking of making ministers, Marbury. The Bishop of Peterborough was never more deceived in his life when he admitted thee to be a preacher in Northampton. Thou takest upon thyself to be a preacher but there is nothing in thee; thou art a very ass, an idiot, and a fool. Thou art courageous, nay, thou art impudent! Thou art a proud Puritan knave, and thou shall repent it."

And so he was sent to prison, child. When he came out he was given another church, in Alford, where I was born. There he continued to speak out, demanding an educated clergy, a clergy fit to guide the souls in its care, and he preached against those who became clergymen only because they were the nephews of powerful noblemen.

And again he was silenced by the Bishops, removed from the pulpit of St. Winifred's, the church in Alford where I was baptized. For many years he lived as a private gentleman, and thought never to preach again. Fifteen years without a church, without a pulpit. Fifteen years to tell his children this story till we knew it by heart. Then, child, there was a shortage of ministers in England, and Francis Marbury was at last given another church, then two churches, both in London. At last he stood again at the altar, and in a pulpit.

Your grandfather never raised his voice in protest again, and he moved with a heaviness I had never seen before, as though the surplice were a harness. And one day when I was nineteen I stood with him in the sacristy of St. Martin's in Fish Street, helping him vest, and with the lacy sleeves of the surplice in his hands, his face filled with blood and he fell down dead.

Nay, nay, grieve not, child, my little one, he got his church, did he not? At long last he got his church, and who is to say that his silence killed him.

———

No one thought so but I.

I think so still.

There is blood on my skirt. I saw it on my hands first, thought it rust, realized what it was, realized I've not cut myself. I've asked them to call Nell. The other midwife was called, immediately was stricken with asthma. They may have to resort to Nell after all, as much as they don't like it; please God she may come. I think they wish me not to miscarry as much as I wish not; if I grow too ill they shall have to let me be at home, and if I grow too ill and bleed to death here in Captain Weld's third-best bedroom they might be accused of poor treatment, of tormenting the prisoner and a woman with child, wouldn't look good at all for them, not at all. Unless they put about a witchcraft story, they could try that I suppose, the usual thing of copulating with Satan or even a lesser demon and then expelling his seed, but these are men of some honor, and Cotton would never be a party to that, never.

Blood on my skirt. Not much, enough to fill a thimble, perhaps, enough to notice, today and yesterday. Will I miscarry? Once before this happened, cannot recall which babe I was breeding at the time, and the midwife at home gave me draughts and made me rest a fortnight and all was well.

Still. Blood. On my skirt. This frightens me more than it should, but even in the midst of feeling ill and contemplating more blood, a sluice of blood warm as tears soaking my skirts — it could happen — their fear amuses me. They don't want me to die on them, that's what.

Will's fear does not amuse me, it took the form of anger which on occasion his fear does and he put his fist through a pane of glass, here in this chamber, after listening quietly and expressionlessly to the news, and after watching me lie here against my pillows like some mockery of Good Queen Bess reclining in her barge, and there was more blood. Not much. Thank God, and they've come to put new glass in the window. Also, thank God, for oh my faith this is a bitter winter.

I sit here now, not wanting much to do anything, I sit and try to hold myself still, and keep the chamber pot nearby. Shameful, I've managed to do this childbearing so well till now, and look at me. I sit and stare, I sit and try to hold like a great sponge my juices within me. I sit with my back to the warm bricks of the chimney and keep the coverlet close about, and even then sometimes I shiver.

They are burning stools and benches in Boston, the wood is so low, and here in wooded Roxbury I hear the constant sound of chains clashing and jingling as they drag more trees from the forest. There has been a great gale of snow and wind, and when the weather clears the sky is hard as an agate and the frost is sharp. The snow lies and lies, overlaid in the mornings with fogs, and on New Year's Day every twig and branch was wrapped round in ice, as if it had grown out of the tree that way and had not yet shed its clear cocoon. Kitty, my little daughter, here on a visit, thought that it was sensible for the trees to grow that way in the cold, thought perhaps that extra layer, like a transparent muffler, kept them warm. I'd never thought of it that way before. Kitty does not know of the blood.

I do not think I shall die, do not think I shall lose this child.

How it is I do not know, but I have always felt a death coming when it concerned a loved one and surely I should feel it with this germ of a child, with myself.

I felt it with Zanna.

I feel something else now, not death near, but the beginnings of a new sort of dread. A dread I've not yet felt while I've been here. Of course there is reason for this: when we go south to our new home in March I shall be four or five months into my term and a bit unwieldy; it will make the traveling harder than if I were not in this condition. But I've put out a fire in the chimney and traveled a hundred miles with child before, and no, that cannot be the reason for this dread.

January. That must be the reason.

*The blackest month of all the year is the month of Janiveer,* they used to say at home in Lincolnshire. *Janiveer freeze the pot on the fire.* I cannot remember such cold, ever. My hands shake. The window breathes chill air. There is frost on all the nailheads all the time, and the boards are warping in the floor. The wind shakes the house and rattles the panes and although I do not go much to the window anymore, I see a world that is brown and crystal and pale, pale, fading away as if the cold is sucking all color from house, land, lanes. I heard that about thirty persons of Boston going out in a fair day to Spectable Island to cut wood, the town still being in great want, the next night the wind rose so high at NE with snow, and after at NW for two days and then it froze so hard as the bay was all frozen up, save a little channel. In this twelve of them got to Governor's Island and seven more were carried in the ice in a small skiff out at Broad Sound, and kept among Brewster's rocks, without food or fire for two days, and then the wind forebearing they got to Pullin to a little house there of Mr. Aspinwall's. Three of them got home next day over the ice but their hands and feet were frozen. Some lost hands and feet and fingers, one died, and two fell into the ice, and a small pinnace was cast away upon Long Island. The men came home over the ice.

This will be happening all winter, people getting trapped on the islands and the bay freezing and unfreezing and people dying of cold, lamed and maimed by frostbite. Only this winter it is worse, worse than ever. And this January is indeed the darkest month of the year; even at noon the light is pale and cool, and the streaks of it that touch the tawny wooden walls and gables of the houses are often a faint blue, like veins in an aged hand.

January: that is why the dread.
That and the blood.


## 13 January

Nell is come. Bless God. She looks stern and solemn and
says little while I lie back against chimney and pillows,
smiling at her, in my queen pose. I cannot make her laugh.
She has brought a case of vials and her still, and has been
set up in lodgings at the inn here; the Hutchinsons are looking after her house in Boston. All she will say is: Well, 'tis
warmer here.

I tell her she looks grim.

She looks grim and says nothing. This is Nell as she is
when she is thinking and when she is protective and when
she is angry, and she is, I suppose, all three. She may be put
out with me for being with child in the first place, and she
tells me I am in my third month and if I don't do as she says,
I shall indeed lose the child. I do as she says, I swallow the
horrid draughts and then feel sleepy and days go by in a
trance, a fog, and all that seems to change is the patterns of
frost on the windowpanes. Much of this time I cannot set
down here for I am not taking it in, cannot recall it.


## 24 January

Thunderstorm with showers of hail and snow. I am between
sleeping and waking, Nell is here, I see her hands passing
before my eyes, moving to the still, to her basket, to me; I
feel her hands and feel the blood in them, warm and jumping in one vein that runs over toward a knuckle. I am quiet,
dulled, as if I have been buried in all that snow beyond; doc-
ile, obedient, like a good child who is good only because she
is sleepy or ill. Passive and aloof from my fate, from jail,
from banishment, I do not wonder what will happen, what
has happened. My mind is empty of questions. I am removed

from my fate, from future and past, and simply know for certain that my back is to the chimney and the wind blows through the walls and Nell is here saving me, spinning me out like a kite to sail on this smooth air in my mind. I want to thank her, try to, she waves it away like flies.

I worry about my family being cold and hungry, I worry about them falling ill, I worry about the wind blowing through their walls and fingers turning black with frostbite, and I worry that they will throw something good into the fire for fuel, like that sea chest, or the armchair, but when I tell these things to Nell she takes my hand in both of hers and tells me not to worry. And I obey.

Then I worry about Nell, about her living in the inn and traveling over icy lanes to this hostile house, and she tells me it is a shorter journey than Boston, a far sight warmer and more comfortable as well, and not to worry. And again I obey. I do not fool myself enough to think that I am trustingly leaving all in the hands of the Lord. I wish I could do that. I am, I know, simply drugged enough so that I do not pace or rise much, so that I may keep this forming child within my body, a house it seems to want escape from, and how odd it seems when I dwell on that. As if my wish to escape this chamber which houses my body has in some way touched so deep inside me it has prompted this babe to wish to escape its house.

I do not know if there is any more blood. Have not asked Nell. Trust her, that is what I do, and stare at her hands and the window, and sleep.

*28 January*

Snowstorm in the night. Nell and I stand at the window, the quilt over both our shoulders, and look out over the houses nearly buried in the snow and the gray figures wading through it with kindling in their arms and watch the gray smoke puddle against the sky, our noses pressed to the glass like children. The world has a new bed. Never have I seen snow like this; Roxbury is a beach with roofs. And Nell and I lean together like sisters, giggling when someone falls, and swears, and staggers on; like sisters in one nightgown, draped by the quilt.

January, I know, comes from a pagan God's name, Janus, who had two faces, one looking ahead to the coming year, one looking back. I do this; 'tis all I am able to do, but whether it is the illness and the drugs or some state of special grace, I look with utter detachment all this month, as one watches a stranger's face in Janus' double mirror.

*1 February*

Dim day, sky so heavy it has wedged itself down over rooftops and around the crannies of chimneys and leans against the walls, leans with a dead drag and a sigh. It is the color of ashes and pewter.

So am I, I am told by one of my children.

Which one said that? Dear God, it wasn't Will, was it, poor man with a jailed, gray-cheeked wife and a cold winter, will he look elsewhere for breasts and thighs to warm him with?

What am I doing, writing nonsense like this onto an actual page with an actual pen?

It is, I think, the beginnings of coming into the world again, such as it is. The world being this chamber.

I have told Nell I want no more medicinals to make me sleepy. However much I would like to stay on that feather-down float that carried me straight over January, I must come to. Must.

Why? Why not sleep till March and they let me out?

Why this penchant for being alert when any sane being would hibernate?

It is because I feel something happening around me and I want to know what it is and I want to be here as things happen. Something is happening in Roxbury, something is hap-

pening amongst the ministers, even in my month of stupe-
faction I knew it, sensed it. And something is happening
with my family. I must be awake for whatever it is that is
stirring. Last night I dreamed I was looking down into a
caldron and its waters were dark but there were down at the
bottom, hands, not pale and ghostly hands at all but hands
with knuckles, callouses, freckles, creases, and these hands
were stirring the water from below, moving slowly slowly
slowly like fish beginning to feed.

Nell says I need the rest and without the medicinals I shall
have to face too many trials, I shall grow restless, and no
doubt she is right. All the same.

And so Nell is pushing me back into the world, into the
state of being awake, a little at a time, each day a bit more,
she is midwifing me, whelping me, borning me, and though I
asked for it God bless me I don't like it. How comfortable it
was, and warm, to sleep and look neither backward nor
ahead. How safe. I feel like a baby who does not want to
leave the womb, and am being dragged by cold forceps. Ah
but Anne, you asked for this, you asked.

The winter is still lying like a shroud over Roxbury. That
hasn't changed. People are ill, as always at this time of year.
That hasn't changed. My children have not been able to
travel to see me because of the weather, and Will has not
been here for a fortnight because of the children, and that I
suppose is to be expected. Ah but it grieves me, it does. It
was better in many ways to lie suspended in sleep.


*6 February*

Here is new grief indeed.

Nell and the others have kept this from me, but now that I
am a bit stronger they could keep it no longer. Again, Nell's
doing: she knows I would not want things kept and hidden
forever, she knows I would break every pane of glass in this

window if I were treated like an old granny forever, and so she told me.

The magistrates and ministers believe that I am still conveying poisonous doctrines beyond this room. Every time some deviation in doctrine crops up they think it be by my hand, by letters smuggled out, or by some other means they do not specify. They suggest Will is perhaps spreading new erroneous opinions he has picked up here.

Dear God.

Nell says that Boston is subdued, and that there is no reason for this alarm; that most people are just trying to get through the winter.

Even so, the court has ordered all the powder and arms taken from Boston to Roxbury and Newtowne.

And grief upon grief, the ministers of Roxbury have punished my friends here, the Reverend Weld and the Reverend Eliot have "lectured, ajoled, admonished," publicly humiliated, exhorted my friends and three, ah the poor men, the poor families, Henry Bull and Philip Sherman and Thomas Wilson have all been cast out of the church. This means that they cannot vote any longer as well, and their families, I hear, are in great distress.

I hold to Nell's hand.

You'd want to know, she says.

Aye. I'd want to know. But ah the pain of knowing.


*12 February*

I have begun to pace; not caring who hears. Nell told me I would do this and has bidden me sit still over and over, but it seems that I cannot do.


*13 February*

I did not realize the change till they asked me to put on a gown and stockings today to meet with the ministers; I have passed so many weeks in flannel shifts, three or four, one worn over the other, bundled in quilts. I am showing about the belly now, far earlier than I ever have; my wrists and ankles and fingers have swelled, and when they brought the glass for me to do my hair the face I saw surprised me: under my eyes are folds of skin, prune-colored, and my face is puffy in the cheeks as if from toothache; my eyes look glazed. If I were called to my bedside I'd call Nell aside for consultation and say, "This woman looks dreadful, what *is* the matter?"

Nell gives me juniper and other things I know not what they are which keep the chamber pots overflowing and yet the swelling and puffiness does not fade. She is worried, I can tell, stern and quiet, and I tell her over and over not to hold herself responsible for my ills.

How poorly equipped I am to say that, after Zanna.

Last night there pushed out from my womb a small bit of matter that looked like a green grape, and was about that size. This is the third time; the other times I was able to conceal this from Nell. But at last I told her, and she looked at me, and at this odd thing, odd as if a star spun down from the heavens and crashed into this room, for a long while. When I woke in the night the candle was lit and she was going through her books, the ones she has from court, and from her grandmother. All is not well with this child I am bearing, but I've vowed not to think of it, not now, not yet.


*14 February*

The ministers again. They want to talk about the resurrection. I want to talk about the meaning of passing stones from the womb the size and shape of green grapes. I want to ask how my family does, I want to know if I can send a note of comfort to the latest victims of these terrible times, the families of Henry Bull and Philip Sherman and Thomas Wilson.

We talk of the resurrection.

Again the ministers. Today they want to talk about the soul. We have little to say to one another, but the discussions held before my illness enlivened me and so I agree to more; not that I delude myself I have any choice in the matter.

I press my puffy arms and hands down through the sleeves of a gown that used to be too large for me, I slide the gown down over my strange and bulging body, I touch, gently, the places under my eyes that are the color of chestnuts. I go down. We discuss the immortality of the soul and spirit. I show them texts which seem to indicate that the spirit is immortal; they take the position that the soul is not, to test me, they say. It is a baffling argument: soul is used so many ways in Scripture, and I take it to mean life, the force of life. Scripture makes this distinction between soul and body and spirit. Round and round we go, in a theological game. Do I think the soul rises, is resurrected with the body, or only the spirit, they want to know. We toss the question like garden greens as if it has no particular meaning; ever since Zanna died I have believed, known, that the spirit, that is the life-force, dies as the body does, and that only the soul lives on. We toss these questions like garden greens in oil, as if we are not speaking of eternal truths here, and I wonder again what it is they want from me. They've done all that is possible for them to do, what more can they have of me?

Or is it this: if I pass some unseen test, will I be given back my good name and reinstated in the community?

Do they want to save me? Make me recant?

But they are not asking me to recant, to save myself, they are simply exchanging views. Laboring with me. But to what end?

The ministers told me today after our customary hour of doctrinal card tricks that John Cotton has cast free of my spell. Their words. Not mine.

Now I know at least in part why Nell has looked so grim, so silently furious.

I will always believe that John Cotton was wronged by his brother ministers. "His colleagues bore heavily upon him and this pressure forced him to recant his beliefs and turn on you," that is what Nell thinks. She thinks that he, out of fear for his position, surrendered all principle.

Well, I told the ministers I didn't believe a word of what they were saying. I swept up the stairs with great grace till I came to the sharp landing where I swayed like a man's baggy breeches in a draught, and when I was safely locked within my chamber with Nell, spent a quarter hour of pain pushing from the womb another of those bits we have come to refer to only as green grapes. This time there was blood. Nell wipes sweat from my upper lip like a barber, quick, sober, no pat, no pets, no licorice. I've no idea what is happening inside me and Nell, I think, does, and won't tell, so we are at stalemate.

Instead of dwelling on easy matters such as blood and death, we pick a fight with each other. We speak of John Cotton.

The ministers say that John Cotton thinks his parishioners used him, gulled him, made him their "stalking horse." He thought they masqueraded as his disciples only to give their teachings respectability. This I cannot believe.

Nell says it's true.

I say it cannot be, I say that he stood by me at my trial.

"And he's repenting of that now," she snaps. As if she's just bitten off the end of thread between her teeth before putting it through the needle.

The ministers come every day now. We talk for longer and longer periods. I feel homely, and thank God I am tall for I am swelled and bulged and show, but inside my head, there, there is movement. Will soon shall be going to buy our new land. I want to write him a letter that he can have with him as he crosses to Rhode Island, and how I wish I could send some charm around him to keep him safe.

But he will be safe.

I feel it.

And how excited he is.

As though he is founding his own colony. In a way I suppose that is what they are doing, the men who have gone into the compact with him and Coddington. Our new home will be either Aquidneck or Portsmouth.

*My Heart:*

I know that you soon shall be readying yourself to go to Rhode Island and plant our new home. Do you feel a very Sir Walter Raleigh? Much derring-do? Do you look at the stars at night and plot your course and pore over maps?

Dearest, if I could only know what you are doing I could see you in my mind and then it would be all right, everything would be all right.

I glance into the lane and see your sweet tousled hair and your crumpled shirt that didn't see an iron this side of Tuesday, I see that crumply shirt, hands clasped behind back coming toward me and though the illusion lasts for only an instant — it is only some man of your height and build and color — while it is there I feel delight, my face is hot and girlish.

Then comes practical Anne: Have you blankets, have your boots been in good repair, and your shoes, please dear one, do not lose any fingers to frostbite, have you furs to keep you warm and the Indian guide you spoke of to speed you on the right way?

I want to tell how I love thee —

I want to tell you to be careful —

Be careful? I make myself laugh. Be careful.

What did the queens say to Sir Francis Drake and to Monsignor Christopher Columbus? Be careful?

My prayers shall be with you unceasingly and I shall trust Providence guide you true on to safety. As I move about this room I shall be with you, swigging water, squinting, pulling up, letting the reins out, watching the trees thud by, I shall be with you, I shall be with you as close as if I were riding with my legs circling yours on the horse.

Will, Will, we are not young now but we have been young together and once again you go to prepare a place for your wife. You pleasure in this, for you it is an adventure. And yet all the while I am waiting for you to accuse me even so, what have you got me into? Will Will Will — can we love each other enough to stretch ourselves from Roxbury to Godknowswhere and in the nights still hold fast? I think we can. My love goes with thee, dear heart. May God watch over us both, and protect thee from all harm, and please remember to put the goose-down lining in your cloak —

*Your loving worrisome Nan*


20 *February*

My hand shakes as I write; Faith has just been to see me, Faith my daughter, the one daughter I could never reach, touch, know.

Thinking it was another interview with the ministers, as happens every day now, I dressed, had my books ready, places marked, when the door opened and there was Faith, standing so still she seemed a painting and the door a frame. Faith, catlike, shoulders coiled inside her mantle, eyes alert.

Faith with eyes that are golden, flecked with green, and that mouth, that mouth that can be anything, that mouth can point like a finger at you, and it can unfurl like a morning glory for a kiss, and it can smile many kinds of smiles.

Faith. A woman grown, twenty now, my eldest daughter after Zanna, Faith who was such a quiet child, golden eyes gazing at sights only she could see, gazing into mirrors, constantly fascinated by mirrors, but such a quiet child that we feared she might never start to talk. August born, she is the only one of my children to be a summer babe: a thundery lass born in thundery weather, growing into a sultry young girl, off by herself while the others played, watching with narrowed eyes. The lass with the smoky voice, always in Zanna's shadow; the one child I could never reach. Faith in retribution.

I embrace her, she pulls back. I can feel her, taut and coiled, holding herself away from me within the folds of wool. She was like that as a child after a scolding, like that for days. But this is not that child, this is a woman grown, a woman I do not know as well as I ought, and I know too it is my own fault.

She has not come to see me before; she is the only one who has not.

I say nothing of it, remembering my mother's wheedling voice as she grew old and accusing.

I say nothing of it, not to spare Faith, it occurs to me, but to spare myself from sounding like a crotchety old crone.
Well.

We sit awkwardly on chest and barrel, exchange amenities.

It is stiff. We might as well be two women forced by overbooking to share a room at an inn.

How cold it is, how I cannot recall such a cold winter . . . I hear my voice scrawl out something of that on the air, hear it making all the sounds and screechings and efforts that a quill does, I can almost see the unwieldy words, written in too large a hand, hanging on the air.

"Aye," she replies.

I ask about the hardships in Boston, how are they managing.

"Aye," she says.

But one hears of so much suffering, of furniture having to be burnt, even some talk of abandoning the spit of land the town is on for a more wooded area, and even so they are managing?

"Aye," she says again.

I shall lose my temper in a moment, this is precisely the way she has always worked me to it. But nay, nay, why should I? I am indeed hurt that her husband recanted with the others who gave in to Winthrop; and I am hurt bad over that. Hurt too that she hasn't been to see me, nor sent word, even if it was out of shame. Hurt too that now that she is here she is so distant, so disapproving, I can see it in the yellow eyes slanting away from me.

"And how is it with you then?" I ask. She can't say aye to that.

"With us? Tom and me?"

"You and Tom, every one. How is it? You first."

She smiles at a string of dried squash.

"Tom and I. Well, we do not do well, as you must guess. Few wish to do business with a Hutchinson, even a Hutchinson by marriage. Tom lacks work, occupation, and we are bound to that house full of brothers and sisters because there are not that many who speak with us."

"Ah my dear, I am sorry it goes hard."

"Are you? We begged you, Mother, begged. We told you we were just starting out, we pleaded with you not to blight our start, our whole beginnings in this new world with a stubbornness over a small theological point, Mother. We begged you, and see how it has come out."

---

"I know, it grieves me to hear it."

"Does it. You sit there and there is nothing that moves, changes, not your face, not your hands, nothing, you are still as formal with me as you ever were."

"Faith, I am sorry . . ."

"Stop. Stop. You aren't sorry so don't say it. Tom and I have a life to live here, and we don't want it blighted, but what of Ned and Katie, they have a baby who will have to wear this name. Do you not think of that?"

"Believe me, I have thought of little else all winter."

"And the others, half of them don't want to leave, they were just uprooted four years ago, they don't want to let go the house, the friends; oh, Father thinks it is a great adventure, and some of the children do, but some are so sad, and Mother, what of them? What of them? Are they not your charge too? As much as your conscience?"

"Ah this sounds like what we went round and round on in September," I say, weary, very weary all at once. "I thought we understood each other — I don't mean approved of each other — but I thought we had understood what each meant. Please, Faith, I cannot go through it all again, not now."

"Ah, because you are ill? You wish to turn me into the ungrateful daughter who makes you ill? You'd go through it again for Sammy if he climbed on your knee, you'd go through it again for Zanna if she were alive. But not for me."

I slapped her. She did not move. We stayed in place, as if waiting to be told what to do next. She sat, I stood. We could hear each other breathing and we could hear the echo of the slap. Then it faded and I wondered if that had indeed happened. I sat down again, tears in my eyes and in my throat.

"Forgive me," I said, my voice hoarse, strange to me. "Faith, I didn't mean that."

She shrugged.

"Try to understand. At least try to understand even if you can't agree. And help me understand why . . . why have you and Tom cut yourselves off from me now, gone over to Winthrop."

"Tom and I have our consciences too, Mother. You are not the only person graced with the ability to search for truth. And besides, I couldn't bear it! We thought we could bear it when we talked about it, when we contemplated what might happen. *We* thought we could. Well, we can't. None of us. Father won't tell you. Nell and Mary won't tell you, my dutiful sister Bridget won't tell you, everyone protects you over here. But we cannot bear it. Father is so occupied with finding a new home and arranging his affairs that he is not with us, the children, much. They look to Ned, but Ned isn't Father. And he has his own family and his own difficulties and cannot give us the help we need. The younger children cry all night. Susanna wets her bed almost every night and Willie has begun to walk in his sleep."

"Stop it, I beg you, don't."

"And there is sickness, they've all been sick with one thing or another, and it goes round and round, the sickness, wearing them down. Nell is here with you so she can't dose them. Mary Dyer helps as much as she can but we've never before had a winter like this, where there's at least two people sick at once, and the young ones distracted and sleep-walking and waking up screaming and the neighbors not helping out of shame for recanting or out of hate, I don't know."

"Ah, sweet heaven! The ministers are an easier lot to listen to than you. You tear me apart, what can I do?"

"You should know."

"What can I do? I can write to each child, I can write out more directions, I admit with this illness I have been writing less than I should be, I can write out remedies, I . . ."

"Nay. Oh Mother, it sickens me. You won't do the one thing that will help us all. Tell them you were wrong, the meetings were wrong, throw yourself on the Court's mercy, bargain with Winthrop, at least try to make it right."

---

"I wish it were so unimportant, I do, dear Lord, I do. I wish it didn't matter and I could take it all back so easily, and have your pain gone — and mine."

"If you loved us enough you'd do it."

"I cannot, dear God, I cannot."

"At least be sorry. Be sorry for what you've brought down on us all, be sorry for starting me and Tom — and Ned and Katie — out under a curse, be sorry for how marked the little ones may be from this, be sorry for all the nightmares and screams and wet beds, be sorry for all the sickness and the lack of any force to hold that household together. You did what you must. At least be sorry, not say, not say, *be. Be.*"

Her back is stiff, I can see the bones running down the middle of her gown like a seam. She carefully presses a palm against the wall, pushes against the wall with all her might. When she takes her hand away there is an outline of perspiration like a leaf print.

" 'Tis just the way it was with Zanna dying!" she says, back still toward me; I stiffen.

"You always cared more for the suffering circle outside your family, didn't you?"

"Why is it I can reach them, and not you, my own child — Faith, give me your hand, please let us make peace, some sort of peace."

"It's too late."

"What did you come here for?" I burst out. "To quarrel? To torment me? For what, Faith, what?"

"I came here to ask you to amend what you have done for our sakes. Because we cannot bear it anymore. Because it will blight my life and Tom's, Ned's and Katie's, all the children who want to grow up and prosper here. I think you must, you must."

"I must do as you think best? Else I lose you, lose my family? Is that what you mean to say?"

"Cold Mother, beautiful, but cold. Must you always turn a

phrase? Remember what happened the last time. Remember what happened the last time you put the good of the town before the good of your family. Remember what happened to Zanna."

"What is the point of bringing Zanna into it?" I scream in a whisper.

"Look what happened. She died. Are we to die as well?" Faith says, flat. "Is it worth it, Mother?"

She goes out of the room very quietly, as if she walks on small cushions, and the door shuts without a sound.

Faith has reason to hate me. Hate me, Faith, curse me, Faith, but come not again with your accusations because they hit too near the bone. *Just as it was when Zanna died, just as it was.*

When the plague came back we tried to keep its white spirit out of our houses by spinning threads across the openings of doors and windows. We all did this, peasant and gentry alike, the lad who sharpened the knives and couldn't write his name and the retired Oxford don, all, all, bowed to the mysteries of the plague. We did whatever we thought might keep us safe, that's what, and if you'd seen pestilence before and you knew it was coming your way, which it was, that year 1630, up from London, you would notice a calm settle over the town, a taut calm and the sky would be bluer and the bells would ring purer for a day or two.

I must be proof against the plague. I've been around it, near it, nursed it, never caught it. No one understands it. If you have seen a town the plague has tunneled through, if you have smelled that odor of bodies lying trussed like chickens, waiting for burial; too many to bury, too many to nurse — if you have ever been around plague, and see it coming again, you want to take precautions. You want to nail down loose shingles, bolt shutters, daub cracks. You must do something, however useless. So Zanna and I spun threads across the openings of doors and windows, that year she was fourteen. She was tall and womanly, could trick you into thinking she looked older, was older. She had a wise face, one of those faces a young lass will have now and then, which is furrowed in a certain way, prematurely, so that even as a child she seems born old. But Zanna was also pretty, blond and pearly, her eyes dark, her lips full. She was my first-born daughter.

Throughout the years of babies and childbearing, she helped me. We lugged them into the sunlight like plants. In the years when it seemed there were naught but babies and dishes and linen, Zanna and I seemed to be struggling along together, sturdy Zanna, coming along with the diaper pail.

And spirit to spirit, never was there so close a bond as this: for we could finish each other's sentences, we read each other's thoughts, we studied each other's books.

We were kindred in a way that comes once in a while, usually not within one's own blood kin. We were mother and daughter, yet more than that; for we were sisterly as well, and sometimes it would all be reversed and she would seem the mother, I the daughter.

When the first signs of plague showed near Alford, around Bilsby and Horsby, we cut the plague stone. We dug extra graves. We did all the good things you do to prevent it from happening. The idea behind this particular nonsense being that if you are prepared, if you go to trouble to disarrange your house, if you invest money perhaps, the plague will laugh at you and pass by. By such strands we, the gentry, the educated classes, hang, right along with the cottagers.

When the plague first began boring holes in Alford, we all trembled. And then it spread and grew and flashed from house to house; and this, they said, was a mild bout of it. I suppose it was.

I stood inside my house with my whole and healthy family and we watched them trundle the dead past the windows in wheelbarrows. The little girl who played in the puddles of sun on my kitchen floor with Zanna, and who grew up to be a beauty and a schoolmate of Zanna's, the lass who leaned over maps with Zanna and me, all of us licking sticky fingers from dipping almonds in honey, dipping almonds in honey because we were looking for where Turkey was, and that gave us a taste for almonds and honey, that girl was trundled past our window. We hadn't even known she'd been ill, she'd gone so fast. Trundled by, her head hanging over the end of a wagon and her long dark hair trailing down the dusty street, so that her face appeared to be caught in a net. Her eyes were closed. Her lips were full and seemed to pout prettily upward for a kiss as the grinding and the pushing and the wheeling went by.

After that I could not stay inside and went to help nurse those who were left alone. It meant going into houses that seemed empty and sometimes they were, it was too late; sometimes a well person was there, frightened, hiding. Bess Wardall went out and worked like that, and so did her sister Alice, many of the women did. The men were digging grave after grave, and carrying and carrying, making more stretchers for carrying. That time I lost my temper at a minister who would not enter a house that had plague, which really isn't unusual, and many physicians would not go either. The shame of it all. Bess Wardall went into the worst of it, I saw her, hiking her skirts up, walking through hog swill, cradling in her arms a hot-water bottle and a jug of thick soup. There were old people who lived in houses where the plague struck who were simply left there, without food, without anyone.

That year there was of course a new specific against plague. There had been everything. One year we burned so much myrrh the house smelled liturgical for weeks. There was always something. Vinegar. Old standby. Incense to cleanse the air. And that year the most outlandish treatment had been recommended, sworn upon: scrubbing with lye soap. So, every day when I came in from, as Faith called them, "the wars," I would first go to a little garden house we had made, a folly actually, with an insubstantial roof, and a pretense of a wall, but we did have it flagged. I'd stand there and strip off my clothes and Zanna would come out with jugs of scalding water and lye soap and I'd scrub off the day. Good way to catch night chills. Fortunately for me it was a warm and mellow September. Zanna laughed as I danced about.

And even with all that work we did, we couldn't seem to help anyone very much. There were elderly people trapped in upstairs rooms, too afraid to come out, and so they died. There were children who were trapped in cellars, there were people that were stuck practically in bare sight that we should have seen and did not see and they died.

And then Zanna took ill. Zanna had a boil the size of a lentil in her thigh. She didn't tell me. She didn't think of it. She was still shaken by the sight of her best friend's young throat exposed to raw public light trundling up the street in a wheelbarrow. Zanna, moreover, was at that time concerned about bumps on her face. She seldom had them; hated them when she did; lumps and bumps were nuisances that might interfere with walking about the village green in the dusk on the arm of some young man, not with death.

But the boil did not go away.

And there was that morning when Zanna vomited blood.

And after that I didn't go out. I was coming down the stair with one glove on, one off, and I saw her bend at the waist as if to suddenly snatch up a pin from the floor, and then her hair coming down, corn-colored rills of hair and more hair, in my sleep it happens over and over, hair rippling down layer by layer like water, hair the color of corn, here, and there, darker than the color of split timber, and as the hair comes down I see that it is coming down because something is shaking the head, convulsing it, repeatedly, and I see the vomit beyond the hair, and the blood.

I don't remember going down those stairs. I don't remember picking Zanna up or putting her to bed. I remember very little of the first day. But what I see endlessly repeating in my dreams are the rippling circlets of hair the color of young split timber, rounds and rounds of it spilling, and the blood.

It was three days. I sat with her and if I closed my eyes, which I must have done, I cannot recall it. I bathed her. I remember heating linen by the fire, or rather having it heated, and covering her with the warm linen in the places where she wasn't being bathed quite yet so she wouldn't get chilled. That careful arrangement of linen, over the shins, over the ankles, over the thighs, then the rearrangement, as if I thought that if I did everything just so, precisely right, if all the edges of all the squares of linen lined up, she would recover. I bathed her because she said she was burning up, I wet her down because she screamed out for water, *cool cool* she wept, crooning the word like a lover's name.

I had a small trough brought, one made for animals but never used, untouched in the back of the storehouse; we could not infect the chamber pots, we could not risk the other children, and the vomiting did not cease. I held her hand, I rocked her with my arms crossed over her chest, bending with her in each shudder, each jerk, and even then, when I saw the blood in the trough and saw the pustule on her thigh, I told myself it wasn't the dread thing, whose name I suddenly could not say or even think, it was only ague, it was only that, she would recover. I steeped herbs. I dosed her. I held her mouth open and poured the brews down her throat and when they came up again I held her.

The other children were kept away, and seemed to make the sounds of distant mice out in the passageways, on the stairs, in the chambers round about us and below. Will came to the door but we felt we must not let anyone in for fear of its spreading through the house and I scrawled notes to the others and gave them to him, and he read them aloud, then threw them on the fire.

Bridget and Faith came also to the door to fetch and carry, their eyes big, faces solemn, no questions, soldiers, they were.

"I love you all, I am still here, your mother, wish I could be toasting with you by the fire and shaking our chestnuts, but Zanna will soon be better and then we shall do just that. Sorry chicks sorry to be neglecting you so but Zanna needs so much care now I'll make it up to you — promise, that is a promise — we'll have something sinful and sweet that will rot all our teeth out at one fell swoop as soon as this is done —"

That is the only note I have of those times. I scrawled it and must have been too tired to give it to Will, and so I have kept it all these years, for that is all I have of Zanna and that time. I wrote many like it. Many. I hope some of them were penned and punctuated a bit better. Will said later the notes frightened him, I am always so careful about grammar and precision and punctuation in writing and here it was all let go. He said it was like a woman who always brushed her hair five hundred strokes before bedtime letting it hang and snarl. He said this from the doorway while I was wetting Zanna's lips with a damp towel, and I heard it only dimly, as though the room were long and a great distance separated us. He seemed to sense that too, he spoke in a clear voice, as if over many people's heads crowding between us in the room.

He came in when I did not answer, and Faith followed him.

Zanna seemed asleep.

I leaned back against him, he kneaded my shoulders.

"If she . . ."

"Nay," he said.

"She has a bit more color today," I said, and stroked the hair back from Zanna's face.

I could see Faith stiffen.

"You'd give anything in the world to make her well, wouldn't you?" Faith said, and though I heard the edge in her voice, hardening those words into a different pattern, I took little notice.

I dipped a rag into a jug of water and moistened the cracked lips.

"I'll do that," said Faith.

She took the jug and rag from me, I sat back, for a moment. The weariness was growing much larger, like a black beast in the room with me; if I so much as closed my eyes, I knew it would carry me off. It was a danger even, sitting down.

It was night. I remember the bright blur the candles made, and the light falling in tawny splinters over the coverlet, the basin, my daughter's sleeping face, and for a moment there was a peacefulness: just the slush of rag in water, the clank of a poker banking the fires, the creaking of the house cooling down, the small night sounds from outside.

"What if she dies?"

"She shan't."

" 'Tis my fault, Will, if I hadn't had her bringing me bathwater . . ."

"Nonsense."

"If I hadn't been out tending strangers . . ."

"Strangers? Neighbors they were, people we knew. What are you thinking?"

"If I hadn't been, if I'd kept to home she'd not . . ."

"You don't know that, this thing follows no pattern."

"If I'd been to home she'd not be ill, I brought it on her."

"Nan!"

"Ah, dear God, Will, I sit here and watch her suffering so."

"You should rest."

"And knowing it's I who's killing her."

"Anne Bridget Marbury Hutchinson!" He jerked me to my feet from behind, spun me round and shook me, looking me in the face.

"Never say that, never again."

" 'Tis true, Will, 'tis true."

He shook me harder, I could feel the rattle in my teeth.

"How dare you be so arrogant." He shook me again. "You presume to have powers of life and death? You do? I go out and deal with tradesmen, weavers, shippers, clerks, buyers, sellers, and you think that you alone could bring plague into this house?"

"You had to, 'tis your living, I didn't have to go out amongst it."

"Didn't you?"

I looked at him straight for the first time, his voice quieter then. But lips still firm, pressed. "Didn't you?"

"Why no, I didn't *have*, that is no one was *relying* . . ."

"Weren't they? If you and Bess and Alice and the others hadn't found those old folk hiding and starving in the lofts of cottages, who would? If you and Alice and the others hadn't tended the parish sick and kept the plague stone filled, who would?"

"Someone would."

"And you, Nan, lying by my side at night, keeping your home, keeping indoors, caring for your own and ignoring the . . . the *horror* out there, you would have slept?"

"Faith said I ought to have stayed to home."

"Faith! She wants a whipping, that lass."

"Nay, nay, she came and tried to tend Zanna and I . . . oh, Will, why am I always so bad with that child?"

"You're not bad with that child, she'd try a saint's patience."

"Willie, Willie, never start lying, you know I'm bad with her, and I wish I knew why. She laid her head on my knee, Will, when she came."

She had stood in the door for a long while till I snapped that she'd best come out or in, she was making a draft, and be quick about it.

"May I come in, then?"

"If you like. Help me warm this quilt then, she's shivering so, it may be best to bundle this over the top of the other, maybe she'll sweat it out."

---

"I can stay all night and help."

"You need your rest, Faith, I'll not have you taking ill too."

"I'll not take ill."

"Hsshht. Don't even say it."

" 'Tis strange with you up here and no one in charge below, it's queer without you."

She had been kneeling by Zanna's bedside, her head against my knee. The pitcher she held slipped from her hands, its handle shattering, the pitcher itself spinning in slower and slower circles, clinking each time, like a clock running down.

I jumped up, I scolded, I may have sworn at Faith, I can't recall, but I was vexed, impatient, worn out and very angry at the clumsiness, though that small voice within me that comments continually reminded me that it wasn't the child's fault.

She helped clean up the spill, she helped change the coverlet, and then stood paralyzed with fright or horror or both in a corner while Zanna gagged and retched and spat blood, all the while I held her.

When it was over, Faith was at the door. Eyes narrow. Hand cocked on hip. Head tilted to one side.

"You won't be needing me anymore, will you then?"

"Thank you Faith, there's nothing more to do just now."

"I'm sorry I was clumsy."

"I'm sorry I snarled."

"Nay, you're not."

"What?"

"You'd do anything to protect her, even turn on me, you would."

"Faith . . ."

"You know, Mother, since the plague came we don't know you anymore. All of us. We don't know you at all."

"Whatever are you talking about?"

"You belong to them, not to us."

"Faith, I've a desperately ill child here, I'm exhausted, this is not the *time*."

"There's never time. Not for me."

"You came to help with Zanna."

"I came to be with you. But it didn't matter, never does."

She swept from the room, her skirts turning the corner an instant after she did; then the door clicked shut.

The last night Zanna was delirious, I held her; she thrashed. I talked to her; she twisted and mumbled. At last she lay still and looked at me, shivering, and never did she take her eyes from mine.

"Zanna, 'twill be all right."

"Cold."

"Another quilt, warm soon, will be all right."

"When, Mama, when?"

"Soon. Rest."

"Frightened."

"No need, no need. Warmer?"

"Frightened. Becky died. We made a pact. Whatever she did I would do, whatever I did she would do and . . ."

"Hsht, hsht, she wouldn't want that pact to go as far as sickness, would she, not if she loved you as a friend, she wouldn't. Put that from you now, 'twill be all right."

"When? Mama. When?"

"Soon."

And I held her and rocked her, and the only thing that quieted her and stopped her from talking, rambling on about Becky and being frightened, was snippets of tradesmen's catches, what they sing beneath your window when they come drumming. It must have reminded her of sale days, crisp blue and white mornings with starch in her dress and new bread on the table, and the tradesmen caroling outside.

*There was a jovial tinker who was a good ale drinker.*
Cold mama frightened.

*He never was a shrinker, believe me, this is true.*
When, when?
*And he came from the Weald of Kent.*
Mama?
Hssht, darlin'. *When all his money was good and spent.*
She nestles against me, shivering.
*Which made him look like a jack-o-lent.*
A rattle of a laugh.
*And Joan's ale is new, and Joan's ale is new.*
"Tinker's tunes," a smile of sorts, lips drawn back from teeth.
*And Joan's ale is new, my boys.*
A chill, we put our heads down, hold firm, weather it.
*And Joan's ale is new.*
All through the night, with the spruce smell coming in on a bit of breeze mingling with the smell of vomit and tallow and illness, and the candles dusting the tables golden as pollen in small circles, and the sheets sighing as we moved against them *New oysters New oysters New Walefleet Oysters.* Her sweat soaking into me, sweat of my sweat, flesh of my flesh, her tears like rain on my hand, tears for Becky, Becky, Becky over and over again Becky and *New Oysters New Oysters at a groat a peck* when mama when *At a groat a peck, each oyster worth tuppence* and the rattling laugh, no voice behind it, the eyes fixed on my face as we rock back and forth, her like a great soft cradle I hold in my arms, so bundled she is with quilts, she is cradle or a cottage thatched with that tawny splintered hair, or a ship, I ask her if she'd rather be a ship and she says, sing, mama, sing. *Wine and cakes for gentlemen, hay and corn for horses,* back and forth, rocking through the night, leaning into the trough shuddering and retching, then up again, wet the lips, rock along *A cup of ale for good old wives* and *kisses for young lasses.* If we can only get through this night when it will be three whole days and nights and they always die within three days if we

can only last we shall outrun it, *And Joan's ale is new my boys, Joan's ale is new.*

At dawn, as the room began to rustle and shift with new shadows, she died. I felt her go, she was in my arms; her breathing had been coming hard, so hard, I was breathless from trying to breathe with her, and then it stopped. I felt her go, and yet I held her. She was a heavy weight against me, one arm swinging out like a great sad rag doll's. I held her and rocked her and sang to her still, my voice a croak, and she still in all those quilts, *Jo-an's ale,* and she still in my arms, and a strand of her hair still pasted against my cheek *new oysters, ne-ew.*

I laid her down.

How keen I feel the empty place, and how sharp, still, is the loss of thee, how hard it is still, missing thee, oh Zanna Zanna, my girl, child of my heart.


## 21 *February*

Every night since Faith's visit I have dreamed Zanna's death over again. And my younger daughter Elizabeth's, also of plague, a scant three weeks later. For months I wandered through a wilderness, picking my way, wandering because I wasn't allowed to stop, but going on without purpose or reason. Familiar things looked unfamiliar. I remember staring at a slotted ladle hanging on a hook before me in the kitchen; I remember scalding my wristbone with boiling water and never noticing the burn till all was finished. I remember rain, then snow. I don't recall much else of that time.

It was then I sought the church for comfort, and found none; it was then priest after priest told me that this was God's way of punishing me for my sins, and I must accept it, or they said it was a test of my faith, and inside my head I thought, I cannot believe in a God who sports with us, cannot, cannot. I needed the comfort I had always found in churches before, the way the light moved, the bells, the smells, the feeling of the presence there, and I felt nothing at all. Nothing to ease the loss, and my guilt, which Will could not seem to reason me out of. For the first time there was no church I felt I could turn to, and there was no one to open the Scriptures to me but the Lord. And so I began that spiritual journey, searching at first, for my own sake, my own comfort, searching for comfort in the Bible rather than in the church itself.

About this time John Cotton, the minister whose preaching I had so loved in English Boston, had fallen ill with a lingering ague, and was absent from his parish for about two years, resting and recovering. After one of my worst and most desperate nights of pacing, weeping, Will invited the Reverend Cotton to our house for an extended stay, recommending the air of the higher ground of Alford. With John Cotton then, I had a companion on this spiritual journey. We talked of many things. We talked of the new winds blowing through the church, and what sort of stand he'd chosen to put up. We talked of grace, we talked of comfort. I will always believe he saved my life.

### 22 *February*

I must now write letters to all the children, individual letters, every day. I should have been told that they were in difficulty. I must now write out a new set of herbal remedies with Nell's help and send them off quick, to Bridget, who will make them up. Poor dear, every time I see her in my mind I see her in that big buckram apron, more of a carpenter's apron, with all her ladles and knives and pockets, and yet I think she likes running the house. At least I used to think so. Was I wrong there as well? *Are we to die as well?* I cannot recant and I cannot consider it, and it wouldn't save my family at all, how would that help Willie sleepwalking.

Oh, dear God, why is he sleepwalking? What if he falls down the stairs? *Are we to die as well?* But in only two months we shall be in our new home in Rhode Island, in a fair new colony and all will be the same as ever. But will it, can it, be the same? *The younger ones I fear are being marked by it . . . there is sickness . . . Willie walks in his sleep . . . it will blight my life.* What if there is more sickness, I shall have to send Nell to tend them but I must not use Nell as though she were a broom or a keg or a convenience. Oh, Will, Will, you are so exalted about the prospect of new land, new colonies, the pot's boiling over and our daughter Faith — can't you talk to her? Words I've said all my life: Will, can't *you* talk to her? *It will blight my life.* If Nell can help me we can get together a selection of herbal remedies good enough to get anyone through the winter, can't we then. And Nell will help, we can use her *Herbal. The younger children cry all night.* Why can't he be at home more? Ah, I know there's the land at Wollaston and the land at Brookline and the land here and there, I know there are certain matters of finance to be taken care of so that we may manage, that is what Will has always been so good at, and because of him we've never had to worry. *We've never before had a winter like this.* Why is Susanna wetting the bed? She never did that, never, she didn't have that trouble once that I can recall. Is Faith speaking true? Of course she is, she'd not be so specific in her fibbing and besides she doesn't fib. *We thought we could bear it but we can't.*

Is this the equation?

If I'd kept to home Zanna and Elizabeth wouldn't have caught plague and died.

If I'd kept to home I wouldn't be banished and jailed and my family wouldn't be suffering.

If I'd not let my circle of concern extend just that far, just past my hem, then all would be well.

Is that true?

If that is true, I did wrong.

Ah Lord, Lord, you ask me to solve dilemmas, you ask me, an ordinary woman with a family, you ask me what you ask of your saints. How can I answer you? How can I know what is right? I thought I knew and now I feel for the first time uncertain, shaken, where is that line between selfishness and principle ah God tell me, where?

### 23 February

The sky is shedding its skin. More faint snow, trick snow, can it be real? The ministers look as though someone has salted them, when they come in for their daily interview with me. Today I ask hard questions, about the resurrection of the body and soul, and show no mercy. I feel ill and angry and grieved.

### 25 February

Bridget has come. Says not to worry, Faith exaggerates, the children have the winter sniffles that is all. What they have every winter. Her cough sounds like a hacksaw and does not reassure me. She asks do I think that I could have kept them from sickness if I were at home? Cocks a brow at me, looks like her father, charms. But I am not there to help, I say. Ah, she says, but you are ill too, and you are one less ill person to contend with. She will hear no more, she says, and coughs and looks thin. Whenever she coughs I feel a rough immediate physical sensation, as if someone were grinding corn in my chest. I can feel the stones rubbing together. I tell Bridget to go to bed and let someone else take over; Katie has the babe, but surely Cousin Gertrude . . .

Nell comes in, looking ominous.

"She oughtn't to be worried," she says.

"She oughtn't to be breeding again," I say.

"Who says that?" asks Bridget.

"Everyone, most likely," I say. "Bridget, dear, go to bed,

please. And I am sending Nell with you. She and I have talked about this, and she misses Boston, and is willing to take you all on for a week. How we'll repay her we don't yet know, but we shall. And when you are all cured, well, by that time, Father shall be back from Rhode Island, and March will have come, a new year begun, and off we'll go."

## *1 March*

Will is in the wilderness. Nell is still in Boston. The ministers thicken around me like pickpockets, they take notes openly now, they'll take any old tarnished opinion, whatever.

March has come in stormy, two days wet and windy, and the mud seems to be sucking people down into the road. I do not go often to the window but that is what I see, cartwheels and boot heels stuck, sucked by the brown mud. *The Angel of the Lord found her by a fountain of water in the wilderness and he said, Hagar, whence comest thou and whither wilt thou go?* Nell says that John Cotton has been speaking against me, saying I seduced him into believing heresies, weeping from the pulpits, begging the congregations' forgiveness for his friendship with me. It began with only that. *And the Angel of the Lord said unto Hagar the Lord hath heard of thy affliction.* My friend. My friend. Last night the Bible flew across the room from my hand to that wall. I must not write lies, I threw it. Hurled it. There has been so much pain, so much pain, and if only I can be certain that it is for some good and worthy reason then I might rest and be at peace; I was certain of John Cotton, I trusted in him; and before that I was certain of my father's church and trusted in it. I am no fool, not easily duped, clever in study, availed of my wits, and yet I cannot now say if I did right or wrong. I knew in September what was right, what was wrong, why is it that I don't know now? Is it like Zanna's death? Did I do wrong to place something higher, some duty, above my family? *And she called the name of the Lord that spake unto her, thou God seest me: For she said have I also here looked after him that seeth me?* Nay I have it wrong. Will is in Rhode Island. I am in the wilderness.


## 2 March

My grandmother always shook her head at March.

> *March'll search ye, April try ye*
> *May'll tell whether live or die ye.*

She would, on occasion, chant that. We paid no mind. It comes back to me now. *March'll search ye.* Well yes indeed, it'll do that. I have not had any poppy juice for some time, nor alerian, nor ladies' slipper, and I see more clearly. I see that they have something else planned for me. Something else they want to do, they've not finished with me yet. They are for some reason, still afraid of me. They are searching me, but for what.


## 5 March

I am far too big with child for the fourth month. A good thing it is that Nell is back in Boston. And looking in on my children. Who are bright and healthy and glossy, according to Bridget. Who are ailing and dispirited and morbid, according to Faith. I wish for the plain truth. I need to know if I have brought some terrible and irreversible harm upon those children. Dear God, I thought it was all solved last September.

I'll continue ill, it's infuriating me, this puking. I'll not have it! What a nuisance, to have to go downstairs to see the ministers with a chamber pot. Never mind. They tell me you can smell spring outside and people are finding birds' eggs in the woods and daisies even coming up, but I don't believe them somehow. I got caught in winter, I am in winter still. I feel cold all the time. Even with my back against the bricks, I'm cold. *Hold up my goings in thy paths that my footsteps slip not.* Over and over it I go, in my mind, while streaks of thick amber light fling themselves like discarded woolen stockings across the floor. Another stone within me wants to push out, I can feel it grinding down some inner channel, through places in me red as the gills on a fish, plummeting down. I've heard of this before, passing stones in urine, and once in a great while in childbearing, and it's never boded well. *I have called upon thee O God: incline thine ear unto me.*

*6 March*

I do a rare thing: cross to the window. When I first came I was there all the time, still believing in the power of that space, that light, that open square. Now I know it has no power. Now I know it merely lets light in, and a bit of cold, there is no magic there. But I cross and watch, because I think it is important to stay in tune with the seasons' change, even if I don't feel them; that's all the more reason to teach myself, force upon myself the knowledge that spring is coming, March has come. A new year. I'll learn it, I will. People toil up the lane as if they are walking waist-deep in water; it is the wind and the mud they are toiling against. I see — or think I see — a well-known, well-loved face — it is. It is John Cotton out in the High Street.

John Cotton, looking gentle and timid and wise. Looking older, worn at the edges somehow. How good it is to see him there, how good to be reminded of his presence. I have banished him from my sight these many months, sent word to him by Will that he was not to risk himself coming to visit me. It would put him into too much danger; more important, Will told me months ago that John feared they would make him one of my daily inquisitors, along with Weld, and he would keep himself from it by whatever means he could.

Never once have I believed what Nell has said of him, that he has turned against me and disavowed our friendship. Nell never liked him, but then she never saw him at home in England in St. Botolph's Church; she never heard him preach there, did not see him forming as I did.

Looking at him again, his eyes so weary, I know that I have been right to trust him. I see no guile in his face; because there is none. They try to trick me by tricking Nell. They would have me believe that all my friends have turned, that all who were for me are against me, and so they hope to break my spirit and rob me of what comfort there is. I shan't let them do it. I shan't be tricked. He is gazing about, from one side of the street to the other; he is trudging round a puddle, he is nearing the house. For some moments I cannot see him, then he reappears in the lane under my window. He is just below me. I see the white of his hair struck by sun so strong the scalp shows through. He stops. He looks up. I lift my hand. But the sun in his eyes, it must be that, or is it the glare on the panes, it must be that, or is it the background I blend with, it must be that. For after a moment he passes by.


*6 March*
*Night*

They awakened me when he came.

It must have been near midnight, I had been asleep for some time. Joseph Weld was in his nightclothes as he showed John Cotton into my chamber and quickly withdrew, noiselessly shutting the door. At first I thought my eyes and wits, blurred from the pillow, were tricking me.

Then, too moved to speak, I crossed the floor and pressed his hands.

"It was good of you to come," I said, and said again.

"This is an unofficial visit." He kept his voice low. "Only the Governor and Pastors Wilson and Weld know of it. I was allowed at last — after many entreaties — to see you only if I promised to speak of certain matters. Any visit of mine has been vehemently opposed all winter . . . *I* have been vehemently opposed all winter by my brethren ministers; their silence at times wounds more deeply than their words . . . A difficult time for us both, then." He smiled weakly, raised the candle he held higher. "I meant to see you yesterday, could not. You look so changed, I was not prepared . . . You *are* ill, worse than they say."

My appearance seemed to shock him greatly, and his shock in turn startled me; I'd forgotten how I might look to someone who had not seen me regularly, as the other ministers have. He looked into my face for a long time without speaking.

Tears came to my eyes. I saw how he too was changed, aged; guarded. He had opened himself to trouble by taking my part at the trial, trouble I had hoped to spare him; thought I had. But no, once again I had brought harm to one as near to me as kin. For a moment I saw John Cotton as he had looked at home in England, robust and ruddy-cheeked and brave, preaching from the pulpit of his beautiful church, St. Botolph's, the changing colors of the light from the jewel-like stained glass windows falling over him like a vestment; and above him the great arching ribs of the nave, as if he stood inside some great fish, another Jonah for our own time, with a silver tongue. I wiped my eyes, saw again the man who stood here in this prison chamber. The contrast was so sharp I felt it as a flash of bodily pain.

He told me he was being pressed to denounce me, and all I had done, said; he told me I must believe in him, trust him, to give him that promise. And he told me something that I might hope for, something I had nearly given up listening for: he would try to intervene to have me released, on the grounds of my illness and being with child.

"With no harm to yourself?" I said.

"No harm." He looked away. "Some — I cannot tell you which — fear you may be brought to childbed here and fear, to speak plain, that you may in childbed die. They fear that then they would be cried down as villains and you glorified as a martyr. Callous, I know, but those who think so shall be the easiest to persuade. However . . ."

"Ah there always is that, isn't there? Some condition? And that is why they let you come? My poor friend, let me hear it then."

"They are quite likely to demand that you be publicly admonished at Sabbath meeting. That may be the only terms they state for your release. Admonition, to remind the community; then your departure."

"Are they yet afraid of me?" I made a dry wheeze of a laugh, my hands on my rounded belly. "Afraid of *me*, still think me a power to be reckoned with? Ah well, let them have their public scolding then. I don't want to bear this child in their prison either."

He smiled at me but in his eyes lay something fearful.

All would be over soon, he said, assuring me he would do what was right, repeating it, he would take what was to him the right way, the right path, the right turning.

He always had done that, I reminded him. For a moment my mind flicked to what Nell had said of him, and then away, I thought again of the ruddy-faced young man speaking out for new and simpler ways to God, from an old and ornate pulpit.

I try to hold that image to me like a comforter as I lie down to sleep again, but whenever I close my eyes all I see is the fearfulness in his.


*7 March*

Hard frost and bright sunshine. The sun has great power now and soon melts off the snows; there are sprouts coming up, poking up like fingers through rags of snows and mud, but it does not look real to me. The winds and mud times of March scarce seem possible — is it not still winter? I have not shifted with the seasons as I am used to doing, I have not made the preparations for the spring wash and the spring cleaning and that monstrous chore that happens twice a year, the shift heavy to light clothing and bedding. I have stayed still . . . and somehow atrophied. I have lost my bearings, my moorings, and time seems mixed up. I must have been here longer than this, it can't be that long that I've been here . . . and I feel it, something is brewing, something else is to come.

*8 March*

Oh it is ill I am, another of these grapelike things passed from my womb in the night, with pain; how could a little thing like that cause such pain when I have pushed out whole infants with less? Pain and blood, and I begin to fear for Nell, fearing that something has happened to her and that is why she has not come. The ministers come. We talk. And every night I rock back and forth and every night I am back in Zanna's room holding her, wishing I hadn't gone from home to serve others, wishing I hadn't done aught to threaten her life. And every morning the quilt is hunched up in my arms.

*10 March*

All night long laboring to pass that stone, that clear grape of a thing that somehow comes from me, and I think I've got up all the blood, but they'll see it on the rags, I suppose. Nay, I'll burn them. If they think I'm sick they'll not let me out, they'll keep me here all the longer.

I know something is wrong. I know it from bearing all those babes and from helping midwife others. I am in the fourth month, but am large enough to be in the sixth. And the child does not quicken. Not a kick, not a wriggle, not a sound. I know something is wrong. Ah God, God, another sacrifice? Is that what this is? Another lamb caught in the bushes? If I'd not been imprisoned would this child within me be growing aright? Did I kill it with this jailing? Did I kill Zanna? Did I? Sacrificial lambs, enough, enough, for though there is no greater gift than a man lay down his life for his friends, that is one thing and that I would gladly do. But I, I am not prepared to lay down the lives of others. Lord, Lord, show me what I did was not that. Show me that I did lay down naught but my own soul, please Lord, please. *Consider and hear me, O Lord my God; lighten mine eyes, lest I sleep the sleep of death.*

Child within me kick please kick scuff your heels against my ribs anything child punch a hole if you like only stir live push up through this dreary time like an arrogant crocus and live.


*12 March*

Faith has sat here all morning. As if she is waiting to be titled or hanged. As if for something. Outside there is a sky too blue, too dazzling for my eyes, and the sun glitters on the wet thatched roof across the street. Faith stares at me, and I stare out the window. *Hide me under the shadow of thy wings,* if we talk we quarrel so we try, it seems to me, to hold off until after mealtimes, when we are fueled. I have passed two more clear glassy stones from the womb and told no one but the pain has made it nearly impossible for me to sit upright and speak with the ministers, and I do not want anyone to know I am ill. So I have taken some of the medicinals Nell left me; she told me which was what, and labeled them, dear Nell, not according to what they are but according to what they treat. A row of vials labeled quite firmly, MUCH BLOOD, FEVER, PAIN, and with a touch of her own wit, the decoction made from dandelions and other purgatives I know well, she has labeled PISS. Thus dosed I can at least sit upright without contorting myself in embarrassing ways, and face clergy, breakfast, Faith, sunlight, dust motes, claps of wind, various memories, doubts, questions, nauseous smell of fish stew from kitchen, children pointing up at me from below, pull of cloth across my belly. Face all this I can. Address it is another matter altogether.

Here comes a woman, a woman of Roxbury I know, walking briskly to stand under my window. It is the wife of one of the men who came to the meetings, one of the poor men who was cast out of the church by Weld and all, for his opinions, one of our friends. Sarah, Sarah! I pull the rag out of the one broken pane left. And crouch in delight.

She smiles up at me in her timid way.

"Sarah!" I cry out. "How good to see you."

"I meant to come sooner." She looks over her shoulder.

"How is it with you? I'm grieved you had to suffer so."

"Aye, 'tis a grievous thing." She pauses. "We are not well, to speak plain. I mean my man's been ill since he was punished so, can't work, and there's people who don't speak to us now no more. There's people who don't like to sell to us no more. There's people who don't like to buy from us neither."

"I am sorry. Oh Sarah, how hard for you." Faith clears her throat behind me in the room.

"Can you see this?" Sarah holds up an egg. "I was sold this because the hens was taken in the night soon after and we have to buy eggs now, see this egg? This come with five others, I was sold them, put them in eggwater to keep, why a nice supper that would make for us, wouldn't it?"

The egg, glowing against the sky, grows radiant, as if Sarah could let go her thumb and forefinger from it and it would go on hanging there against that patch of sky she's set it off on.

"Good price, sometimes good things come."

"Aye, Sarah, sometimes good things come. You've been brave."

"Last night Richie, the baby, he drinks the eggwater, he doesn't know any better, he just lapped at it and he was ill. I smelled it, smelled the eggs. Rotten. Rotten. Rotten."

She says that word so many times I think it begins to be a sort of a chant for her, or for me; she gathers the word deep in her throat and coughs it at me, over and over. Rotten.

"And I think," she says, after a while, after she's spat the last of the *rottens* from her mouth, and paused for breath. "I think what Mr. Dudley said at the trial all those months ago. He said, three years ago we were all at peace. At peace. That we were. Things weren't grand and fancy, but we were getting from one day to the next. Now we have troubles and I can't help but see, Mistress Hutchinson, that they all come from you. You let us come into your house, you showed us a way of believing and worshipping that was a comfort, but you brought us down. You ruined us. Because of you my family is outcast here, worse off than we were at home in England. Outcast. Because of you, my children can't grow up proud of their name, their name will always be an outcast's name. Because of you my man is ill and people think it doesn't matter if they steal from scum like us and the hens are gone and what am I going to do."

She is crying, her face ugly with the tears, wiping them with a dirty hand that makes the water run through mud patches and soot, her lips pulled back from her teeth, and she keeps crying.

What can I do, what can I do? I want to help her, I want to defend myself, I want to . . . she throws the egg. The rotten egg. It smashes against the window, doesn't come in but some of its yolk clings to the window, a splattered golden eye, membranes, glossy, stands on the window, and the smell. Someone leads her away.

I turn and look into Faith's eyes; I turn away.

The pain is worse. Another dose. Vial marked PAIN. Cannot get egg off broken window, tried and cut my arm on the glass. It is cooking in the sun, stringy yellow tendrils that cling to a patch about the size of a cup's bottom, whitish, as if someone sneezed there. Staring at it, must stop.

Sarah, Sarah — how many of you are there? How many have been hurt now? And is it wrong I've done, truly? *Perhaps*, there's always that *perhaps*. It grows larger. Perhaps whole lives were scarred, not helped, because they crossed mine. Perhaps my meetings were vain and foolish exercises and perhaps the ministers are right about me and perhaps my daughter is right about me.

Sarah, what can I do to undo your trouble? If I could take the blame on my back, would I? Am I to blame?

Was all this for naught?

Or worse: for the hurt of others?

Dear God, I no longer know. I used to know so clearly, so surely. Now all is dark. There is a mist coming down now over the town. Late afternoon, dusk soon. House quiet. Womb silent. *How long wilt thou hide thy face from me?* Don't know what they're planning but it cannot be good. Faith is trying to get me to do something, but I do not understand why she says recant, for there is nothing to recant of. *How long shall I take counsel in my soul, having sorrow in my heart daily?* I wish I knew if my husband and children were well and safe, I wish I knew how Sarah will manage, I wish I knew if she is right. *How long shall mine enemy be exalted over me?*

The light is fading, leaking out of the room, and soon I won't be able to see the egg so clearly. Soon it will be supper, chamber pot, quilt, candle, sleep.

*I have trusted in thy mercy.*

But did I do wrong?

Am I a bad woman then, as they say?

Have I ruined lives, and more lives, and still more lives?

And stunted the one within?

*My heart shall rejoice in thy salvation. I will sing unto him because he hath dealt bountifully with me.*

The candle and I, alone; it is night. No egg visible. I and the candle. We sit against the bricks, candle and I, and this burden within me presses against my backbone. There. Better. All right, Anne, all right. There will be no crying or coming apart here, there will be —

*Oysters new oysters new oysters*
even if I am a bad woman who's done everything wrong
*New Oysters New Oysters Walefleet Oysters*
*At a groat a peck each worth a tuppence*
*And Joan's ale is new, my boys, Joan's ale is new.*


*14 March*

I am going home.

Home.

I cannot believe it, they only just came and told me. Tonight the marshal will come with my son Ned and carry me home. Thank God. So suddenly it is over.

The children are in Mt. Wollaston, at the farm with their Wheelwright cousins, and Mary Wheelwright overseeing all; she will not go to join her husband till spring. All the children except for Ned and Katie, his wife, and Rich and Francis, who went to Rhode Island with their father, and Faith and her husband Tom. So I shall go back to a near empty house for one night, and thence to Wollaston, and then we will all begin the journey to our new home. Or so I assume; the message from Ned was so short; it simply said he would be coming for me and that they had almost done with the packing at home and Father has indeed negotiated with the Narragansetts for a piece of land on Aquidneck, Rhode Island.

And Captain Weld came and told me that I would be expected home by the marshal tonight after dark, so that there be no disturbance, and that was all he said.

I have laid my few things away slowly, carefully, thoughtfully. After the first rush of blood to the head and joy to the heart, I feel suspicious. It is too easy, too quick, and there have been other troublesome signs. For the past week I have been entirely alone. No ministers; they abruptly ceased coming. No more from family, but I expect that is because they are all too busy packing. Ned's note that Will had bought the land and was preparing a home for us in Aquidneck came a week ago, soon after my last entry.

But there is something more, some public humiliation I would guess, something coming; I feel that the ministers are somehow unsatisfied. They haven't had the chance to fully justify themselves or avenge themselves on me for attracting members of their congregation to my home. But what is coming I know not, and I fear it; I keep remembering what John Cotton said about a second public admonition. What more can they do to me?

I lay away my handkerchiefs, my nightshift, my Bible, my lavender water, my vials of medicinals. In a wicker hamper I lay them: handkerchiefs folded twice, then over once, nightshift folded in thirds, the Bible on top. In a smaller basket that rides the folds of white nightshift in the hamper, I lay the vials of medicinals, of scent, I lay a key I found in the pocket of my gown, though I know not what lock it fits; and the other books that have kept me company here; and the soap-ball worn down to a third its size, still smelling faintly of bayberry, I wrap in a cloth and lay there and the large vial of lemon-wash and the small twig-brush for cleaning the teeth; I wrap them and lay them down the way we used to lay presents out for Christmas, gift at every plate. I lay them there and look at them a while. Then I close the lid. And stand, and wait. Outside there is a growling sound, as candlelighting time arrives and I, with my small candle, sit here, writing to pass the time, or make something of this time before I go, I hear it. It sounds like a rumbling, of distant thunder or the clearing of many throats; there is a restlessness outside. I do not go to the window.

I do not go to the window because for each day of this past week the wife of the Roxbury man who was cast out of the church, Sarah, has stationed herself beneath my window. She has not thrown any more eggs, she has thrown nothing at all, said nothing at all, she just stands there, as if that is her work, from dawn till dusk, to stand beneath my window, and because I find it unbearable to look into her face or even glimpse from the tail of my eye that still form, I do not go to the window.

Dark. Supper's over downstairs. I hear my son's voice below me in the hall. And another voice, deeper, most likely the marshal's, and then more voices, men's voices, a steady rumble beneath my feet. Sweet Heaven, why won't they just come and unbolt this blessed door? I feel that if they don't I shall want to kick it in. The growling outside is louder, that sound of many throats, but even when I peer out at the corner of the window I cannot see anything. There is no room, it's deep dark, I cannot see but feel some restless even malicious presence outside.

A knock at my door: I am on my feet and at the door in one motion, saying, "Aye."

The door unbolts. Captain Weld enters, to my surprise; not my son, not the marshal. We exchange stares, then he clears his throat and, much too loud, says that he wishes me a good evening and hopes that my stay here hasn't been too discommodious. I incline my head, wish him a good evening, and say I am ready to go down.

This is all very odd. He is moving as a squirrel does in quick jerky motions, and then freezes.

Clears his throat again. Says fast and formal that tomorrow being Thursday Lecture Day I am required to appear before the Massachusetts Clergy in Boston Church before I take my leave of the colony, as the elders find it necessary, and the lecture will be two hours earlier, at ten o'clock.

Ah. It has come, what I thought, a public admonishment, something of that sort. Well, I suppose I can bear that, an hour's harangue in public, chastisement before all, and then I am free.

"We shall have to go out the back way," he says. "Your son is here and the marshal, and they will take you with the constables by cart over the neck. Arrangements have been made that the gate be raised in case it be past nine when you reach it. We shall have to go out the back, and we shall have to hurry."

It is so dark in the chamber I cannot see him except in silhouette but I can smell his sweat, sense fear; and then three or four rocks, I cannot remember, crash in through the window, and I hear the growling from outside more clearly. There is a crush of people in the High Street, must be, but they are almost silent and why can't I see any faces? Captain Weld tries to hustle me from the room, but I pause, feel for the candle in its holder, and the tinder box. It is so dark here with no lights and no moonlight from outside we'll never get down the stairs without a light.

"No need to break our necks going down," I say, as the tinder catches, and the candle lights. I go down ahead of him, holding the candle high, step by step by step, each one loud, crashing through the house, and in the dimness below I see faces: the Welds, my Ned, the marshal, and the constables, four or five. The noise is louder down here. There is a mob outside and they are shouting something.

Ned's hand is under my elbow. We go to the window, to the edge of it, and peer out. Now I understand why I couldn't see them. They've all blacked their faces and hands so no flesh catches the light. Eerie dark figures, crammed together, without any lights, arms linked and from their mouth one word: *Jezebel. Jeze-BEL-Jeze-BEL-Jeze-BEL.*

We wait. As if for a letup in a thundershower. We wait for the mob to quiet down. So I am told. The Reverend Thomas Weld confers with Captain Weld, they confer with the marshals and the constables, and Ned hangs about the outside of this circling of male shoulders, trying to hear what he can.

There is no one round the back, we could go in a cart down that lane if someone could keep the crowd distracted.

It is decided: The Reverend Thomas Weld will go out to talk to the crowd, and meanwhile we will steal out the back way. They are bringing the cart round. I can hear the chanting, louder now, it comes in waves, pressures the ear. The voices sound thick, dense, like the pitch on the faces, and the dark noise mounts as I rise. I put out the only candle. How dark it is, all at once, here inside, how dark it is round back, and how dark it will be all the way to Boston, even with lanterns on the cart. I step forward gathering my shawl about me, tucking the edges in firm, as if it were cold out, with a wind. But it is against the darkness I gather my shawl: not the cold, not the wind, but the drumming dinning dark.

# PART III

## NELL BENEDICT'S NARRATIVE

*June, 1638*

BOSTON

*I*'ve not much longer for the telling of this tale.

The General Court of Massachusetts Bay has placed me under suspicion of witchcraft and advised me to quit the colony with all due haste.

As if I needed the advice.

In the meantime I am forbidden the questioning of religious matters in private or public, and banned from the "meddling" — as they put it — in surgery, physick, plasters, potions, and oils, within their jurisdictions. A neat way to shut my mouth and stop my way of earning my bread all at once.

Meddling. Indeed.

How badly they want us midwives gone is clear enough; Jane Hawkins is banned as well. They know all too well that we have the trust of the women here in ways they never can; for that they fear us, and fear our continuing to speak of Anne's ideas behind doors they cannot, as men, open. I was wondering how they would go about punishing Anne's friends amongst the women, those who have not left the colony or fallen silent or repentant alongside their husbands. They couldn't disarm or disfranchise us as they did the men — and crying witch has always been the easy way.

But 'tis cheap. Pah, cheap. And dangerous.

We all know that, we've seen enough of it at home in England.

---

Everyone is afraid now. Casting out Anne has not brought the peace promised by Winthrop and the elders. Indeed some think it has brought a variety of misfortunes down upon us, the chief one occurring four days ago.

The earth shook in the afternoon for about five minutes and there was a constant drumming noise everywhere as if a mighty army were marching upon us. I saw ships in the harbor pitch from the water, I saw people fall upon their faces and forget and cross themselves in the old Romish way, I saw a crackline appear in my kitchen wall like a long strand of hair suddenly blown against it.

The elders proclaim that as the quake rushed from west to east, it was the wake caused by the exiled New England Jezebel: meaning Anne. A clear sign of Providence, they say.

The people, many of them, whsiper that the quake rocked the colony as punishment for driving out a true saint of God, also meaning Anne. A clear sign of Providence, they say.

To speak the truth, I never was much for reading signs and portents and even if I had the gift I'd not say word about that now — I never was much for begging extra trouble and I've enough as it is. I'd best turn to the work at hand.

It was early April when I began this telling.

It is now the fourth of June.

My departure has been delayed by fever and ague which spread this spring through town; my recovery has been slow. I had to unpack much of what was laid away but now that my strength has returned I have done almost all of it up once again. I shall be finished well before tomorrow when the carter comes.

What I must do right now is find a length of stout twine for hoisting the chests and fold the last of the linen for packing and tell you what happened when Anne was let out of prison a year ago March.

And I'd best be quick about it.

*W*hen she walked into Boston Church, past the gawkers pushing in at the back and the shoulders layered four and five deep and the staring blur of faces, walking down the center aisle between the rows of raised heads, I felt a shock go through the crowd. It was the same shudder we first know as children at a fair when an acrobat seems about to fall or a costume flares near a sputtering torch.

Boston had not seen Anne since her November trial, since imprisonment and strain and the difficult childbearing had hollowed her face and thickened her body, and made so strangely puffy the long expressive hands. I cannot say how many stared out of concern, how many out of curiosity: her truest friends had gone with Will to Rhode Island, leaving few openly in sympathy with her besides the Hawkinses, and the Dyers; I could see Mary's bright hair halfway down the aisle. And I could see Dinely's balding head across the aisle from her on the men's side. I was standing at the back, feeling a strong aversion to this proceeding, not wanting to make myself a part of it, not wanting to be there at all. I stood there and looked at neighbors I no longer knew.

A list of one hundred doctrinal errors was read aloud, a new list compiled by the ministers from their meetings with Anne in prison.

Anne said: "These elders came to me in private to discuss

certain points. They promised before God that they came in good faith, not to entrap or snare me. How is it that now they turn around, make public our discussions and use them against me? By what rule of Holy Writ, I ask, is this done?"

"Does Mistress Hutchinson accuse us?" Newtowne's Pastor Shepard demanded. "Does she accuse any of us of breaching a rule of Holy Writ?"

"I have not accused anyone of anything, sir." Anne's voice was weary. "I did but ask a question."

"I would have this congregation know that the vilest errors that were ever brought into the church were brought by way of questions." Shepard's voice rose.

That day passed in a stream of words, untouched by air and sun.

I stood in the back for three hours.

I sat on a stool for six more.

As ritualized as antiphonal prayer in the old church the trial proceeded: question, response; question, response; quotation of text, refutation of text, the ministers' voices, her voice, theirs. *These opinions cannot be borne.* Their long black gowns dragging along the floor, forked Geneva neckbands glossy with starch. *This shakes the very foundations of our faith and tends to the overthrow of all religion.* Thin light falling in squares across the shifting gowns, her shoulder, the pastor's cheek. *Sister, do not shut your eyes against the truth.* Outside a rising wind, ice shells crackling off the trees, pelting the wall like stones. *Acknowledge your poisonous errors.* It began to grow dim in the meeting house.

Only four of the supposed "errors" had been dealt with.

"If the church be satisfied," Pastor Wilson spoke, "and if it be convinced in its judgment that these are Errors and that these Errors are hers, let them express it by holding up their hands."

Ned Hutchinson stood up to intercede. "Sir, if, as my mother's son . . ."

"You are not to be led by natural affections." The Reverend Davenport cut him off.

Again Wilson's voice sounded: "If the church conceive we ought to proceed to admonition we will take silence for consent; if any be otherwise minded, let them speak."

Again Ned rose, again Davenport silenced him.

Wilson once more put the question. "If any be otherwise minded, will they now speak?"

From the back of the meeting house came a voice that swung our heads round: Tom Savage was stepping forward to speak.

"I am not yet satisfied," he called out. "I have tried to be fair and not be partisan out of family loyalty, but I cannot agree with what you are trying to do here. There is no rule in Scripture for the admonition of a member who has only sought light on certain matters. I cannot consent that the church should proceed yet to admonish Mistress Hutchinson for this."

From the congregation other voices spoke, protesting that she had only made inquiries into doctrine, rather than declaring new truths.

Before anyone could speak further it was quickly decided to place under ecclesiastical admonition both Ned Hutchinson and Tom Savage, alongside Anne. The congregation went silent; a chill seemed to fall over the meeting house. Clear it was that anyone speaking on Anne's behalf would suffer for it.

Pastor Wilson stood up, an air of energy and animation about him I'd not seen before.

"It is indeed very meet to lay these two brethren under admonition with their mother. The whole church, by its silence, consents to the motion. And now, Reverend Teacher," he said, turning to Cotton, "as one whose words may be of more respect to her than ours, and so sink deeper, we ask you to deliver the admonition."

John Cotton stood, plainly startled and distressed. He moved slowly from his seat to the pulpit, his eyes averted from Anne; the edges of his ears pink. He cleared his throat and began, first addressing Tom Savage and Ned Hutchinson.

"You, her sons, must not hinder the work of repentance in her soul; drawn by natural affection you may, like vipers, eat away at her. In the cause of God one must disavow both father and mother." He turned to Anne, cast her a long glance, and spread his hands out, as if for support, on the pulpit.

"And now, Sister." Cotton turned to Anne. "Let me address myself to you. May the Lord put fit words into my mouth and carry them home to your soul. I would speak it to God's glory that you have been an instrument of doing good amongst us . . . He has given you a sharp apprehension, a ready utterance and ability to express yourself in the cause of God. The Lord has endowed you with good parts and gifts fit to instruct your children and servants and to be helpful to your husband in the government of the family. But your unsound opinions outweigh much of the good you have done. Especially do I fear the consequences of your recent reflections. Therefore, I do admonish you and charge you in the name of Christ Jesus, in whose place I stand, that you would sadly consider the just hand of God against you, the great hurt you have done to the churches."

As John Cotton descended from the pulpit, the last light had drained from the meeting house. It was cold. It was long past suppertime; no one could see well, or move without stiffness. The church had spoken. The ministers had delivered their admonition. She had held them off for six and seven and nine hours. For a moment I thought it was over. For a moment I thought she had won.

The ministers sat conferring at their table, as an expectant stir passed through the church and people began gathering themselves together to leave. All at once, arrowing through the rustling of cloaks and capes, came Pastor Wilson's voice.

"We are still in session here. Our purpose is not yet fulfilled."

Again, silence.

"We are not satisfied that Mistress Hutchinson is aware of the magnitude of her errors. Her soul is in mortal danger. Therefore we deem it fit that she be returned to prison for further exhortation by the ministers."

I felt a ripple run through the congregation.

"Mistress Hutchinson shall be transferred from the custody of Mr. Weld directly to that of our faithful brother John Cotton, where she shall remain in seclusion until we are satisfied."

God knows we weren't expecting that.


For a week we were not permitted to see her; no one was. All we were told was that Cotton was laboring to save her soul.

I wondered what Anne was going to do. Perhaps they were laboring to come to some agreement then, that would prevent further activities on her part, and save Cotton's honor, for his. It was a week of watching and waiting, and of great worry. I wondered how, in her bodily condition, she could stand the hours of arguments, appeasement.

Cotton's house was looked upon, that week, as a house of illness. People stared at it, dropped their voices when they passed it, moved quickly to leave it behind.

The shutters were closed. The gate was latched. An unnatural stillness hung about the place. But for the smoke blowing up the chimney and the woodpile dwindling, one might have thought the house was empty.

We went through three weeks clinging to everyday chores, going hand-over-hand from lighting the fire to drawing the water to damping the fire to lighting the candles.

We went about close-mouthed, tight-lipped, as if we had sent all our strength and life to Anne in her struggle at Cotton's house. In that week I knew for the first time in years of midwifing what a father's vigil must be.

*C*ustard!" said Anne.

We stood amazed, gazing at her as if she had just called out for Lizards! Diamonds! Manure!

We stood amazed, those first few moments of the evening she came home from prison, we stood and drank her in — because we'd feared they'd not let her out after all or transfer her yet again to another minister's house; and because it seemed so long since she'd been here amongst us. Despite ourselves we had forgotten the sandiness of her voice, the turn of the nose, how thick the lashes, sparse the brows, candlelit the gray eyes — all the small things about her we had, every day in ordinary times, seen and heard; and yet not really seen, not really heard. We stood there taking her in again, as she whooped her answer to our inquiries regarding supper.

"Custard, craved it, all this past week I did, all this winter long, ah dear God, home, I'm home, I am."

She stood in the dim great hall of her own house again, her hands on her hips, looking older, looking unwell and clearly with child, but looking like herself after all, regal and stringy and strong, amusement and tears in her eyes.

Never mind the marshals outside the gate.

She knew about them.

———————

Never mind the dimness of the place, all but three candles laid away with the family's entire belongings, packed up and awaiting the carters next day.

Never mind the stools and the benches stacked waist-high and the crates and the chests bound with twine and the table standing about looking uninvited.

Never mind the silence, the emptiness of the place, Will off in Rhode Island readying the new house, the children off in Mt. Wollaston with the Wheelwright cousins, the cats gone and all the livestock but for some hens, sold, called for, gone.

Never mind that this was the last time she would ever sleep in this house.

She knew about that, all of it.

Not much of a homecoming, it seemed to me, so furtive, so few of us, so dark. But it seemed enough for Anne.

"All's well now, all shall be," she said, a little too fast, a little too bright, "No talk of prison or ministers or anything weightier than custard tonight. We'll be a Boston family again, and a merry one, for one last night."

She went through the house passing her hand over every near surface, peering into every chamber, every cranny, like a child returned from a summer with relatives. Everything seemed important to her: the mumblety-peg scars in the floor, the burn mark on the wall from the birthday pudding, a floorboard's familiar creak, a glance from an upstairs window, a nick in a downstairs door.

Bridget wept when she thought no one was near, wept in the kitchen.

*No tears*, I hissed, and shook her, *for this one night no tears*.

Bad enough welcome as it was, I told her, only herself and me and Mary Dyer, Ned and his Katie — the numbers allotted by the marshals — only a cold meal and a dark house; we had better be a merry lot to make up for it and we had better get the supper on this minute and that had better be the end of it.

And so, in that dim and hollow house we seemed to be

haunting, we gathered everyone together and laid out the food and began making Anne's custard.

Not an easy job was it, what with the lack of light and the cooking things packed and the baskets of foodstores who knew where. We pried up lids. We knifed through cording. We rummaged in barrels. We startled one another in the dark, lurched into things and knocked things down, we swore out loud. And how we did laugh, fits of laughter welling up through the musty rooms as we broke into crates, ransacked chests, feeling naughty, feeling like children left to their own devices while the grown folk are away. And like children, the messier we became, the more we spilled and blundered, mistaking salt for sugar, chamber pot for kettle, the greater was our laughter; laughter that floated on the dusty air like distant music from another time.

Someone began a whistle that turned into a hum into a tune *All of a misty evening* and the sound threaded through the room as Anne found a pewter dish and found a recipe and Mary fetched the milk pans, *a misty misty evening*, and we were banging the spice and drinking the ale from the keg kept out for us; the cups nested in our hands, the fire flirted with us and pranced, pine shavings atop split oak flashing white, *with a how do you do and a how do you do*, the room drew round us, warmer, the ale was quaffed again *all of a misty day* and the laughter seemed not so distant.

Bridget held the recipe up to the firelight and read aloud:
". . . let the cream just boil and pour it boiling hot with . . ." She looked at us, horrified. "Sack sherry?"

"Here it is," Anne said, a leather bottle in one hand, a cone of sugar in the other.

". . . sweeten to your liking and shake in a little nutmeg . . ."

"Hard as a rock," said Kate, still banging a ball of it.

". . . stirring all the while, and once the cream is set on a few coals of a soft fire, covered, never stir it lest the curd break. Take then sixteen egg yolks — *eggs*."

We all looked up, horrified, having neglected to think of that, but there were still those hens out in the back, waiting to be fetched next day.

"We live in hope," said Anne.

With a low-wicked lantern and a dark cloak, I left them all at the hearth, hoping to avoid the marshals as I went off to the coop. Like a thief I felt, dodging about, holding my breath, under the glare of those hens.

I didn't hear the half-door open because of the clucking.

I didn't see him at first because I was reaching into a nest.

"Hsshhht, don't scream for God's sake."

"Hell's fire — *Dinely.*"

"Saw your light."

"Scared me queer."

"Sorry."

Dinely and I have been formal and awkward with each other since he publicly repented his association with Anne and "the opinionists," and saved himself being disarmed and disfranchised. We never spoke of it. We never seemed to meet anymore. He never came round our house, nor I his. I miss him.

"I sneaked over, the marshals never saw," he said. "Came to tell you what I heard about tomorrow. Understand; no one knows I'm here, no one must know, you've not seen me, spoken with me, nothing."

"Oh Dinely, don't, we've always trusted each other." To hide the tremor in my voice I snapped, "Besides, nobody of any importance here would believe a word I said."

He tried to laugh.

"What are you doing here, Nell?"

"Preparing custard."

"Indeed?"

"I am." I held up an egg. "What's it to you?"

A long hard silence.

"I know what you must think of me," he said.

"You don't."

"What else could I have done?"

"You've no reason to explain to anything to me."

"Alice, the children, shares of land, the house, the shop — how could you expect me to risk it all? For conscience. For a stance, a position."

"No one expected anything," I looked away.

"The rich ones, they can leave and plant a new colony and name it after themselves while they're about it, easy for them to have consciences."

"I am leaving," I said, unable to stop myself. "The Dyers are leaving. The Hawkinses are leaving."

Another stretched silence.

I gathered the rest of the eggs, not glancing up, while Dinely watched by the door.

"I'd best tell you and get back."

"Well then."

"It won't be what you think tomorrow in meeting, just a bit of time taken up with another mild reproof to Mistress Hutchinson. It won't be just a slap on the wrist."

"What are you saying?"

"She's not going in there for simply another public admonishing."

My lips were numb. "What then?"

He kept crunching back and forth over the straw.

*"Dinely."*

He stopped and stood still, hands behind his back.

"I want you to know," he said, tight and fast, "there's many of us that don't hold with what they've done, what they're about to do, who remember her well, but we simply cannot . . ."

"Spare me this, say what's to happen."

He took a breath. "They mean to excommunicate her. Another trial. Ecclesiastical. And that's how it will come out. Excommunication."

I stared at him.

"Why?" I said at last. "For God's sake, why that?"

"They want an example. And more. I can't . . ."

"Go *on*."

"They want her cut off, severed, as they say, not just from the body politic but from the spiritual body, the one established church here excepting the Plimouth Separatists. They want everyone to see that, I think, so there won't be any lingering, ah, loyalty, secret following. She was so loved. Before. I think they fear that still."

"They want her disgraced, ruined." I spat. "A bitter thing that is. And how calculated, they let her out just when Will would be away."

" 'Tisn't so bad as you make out; she's banished already as it is, that's the worst of it."

"There you're wrong. For Anne excommunication is far worse than banishment."

"Oh come, Nell. 'Tis a ceremony, a word, she won't be here to be barred from the meeting house door. It can't harm her family nor turn a hair on her head."

"Dinely, Dinely, didn't you know her at all? Can you cast a wick from a candle and expect it to light? To be cast from that spiritual hearth, that center, would be for Anne, I think, a kind of death sentence. They can't do that to her, 'tisn't necessary, perhaps you're wrong, perhaps they'll only go through the pomp, splendor, terror, and have done?"

He shook his head.

"Surely something can be done, something, even now?"

He shook his head again.

We stood in silence for a while. At last he turned to go.

"You've no right to judge me, Nell, she'd be the first to say it."

"True, I've no right."

"Tell her I wanted her to know what she was walking into."

"I will."

He opened the half-door.

"Dinely. You're wrong about one thing. She'd not be the first to say it. It would be someone like you."

He half-smiled, let me have the last say, and trudged off across the straw.

They were singing wassail songs and stirring the cream over the fire with the stem of a clay pipe for lack of spoons, they were gathered round the hearth calling instructions and banging spice and laying more wood down on the andirons. A bit of spruce with the greenery still clinging to it had been tossed across the table, reminding me of the old days at home when we still celebrated Christmas and the house crackled with a festive feeling, as this house did, despite all, this night.

I came in quietly and stood watching them for a moment: each face in silhouette, carved from the darkness, and strung across the hearth like mummers' masks, bobbing and dipping as in another time, another land, when the mummers came singing carols, tinkling bells, bearing gifts. The smells of spruce and nutmeg and warm milk came over me, smells that meant all was well and merry and safe. My eyes filled.

"Here's Nell," Mary said, or Kate, or Bridget, a reedy expectant voice winging out from that panel of brightness framed by the mantel. "Here's Nell now, luck?"

"Eggs," I said, flat.

The eggs were admired. I was congratulated. Mary was taking her turn with the stirring, Bridget was cracking the eggs and singing softly, under her breath, *Wassail wassail all over the town*, and Ned put another log on as the yolks floated rich and golden on the simmering cream. *My bread it is white and my toast it is brown.* A freckling of nutmeg over cream and eggs made it beautiful, too beautiful. *A wassailing song I'll drink to thee . . ."*

"Stop it, Bridget," I snapped, rather than weep.

Bridget, her eyes showing hurt and bewilderment, stared at me, I who had shaken her in the kitchen and demanded merriment of her. "Never mind me," I said after a moment. "Nasty old woman I am, cranky when the weather changes. I'll go find spoons."

Long after the fire was banked, the custard eaten, everyone gone to bed but Anne and me, there were no tears, nor any mention of the next day. We walked about the house again, slower this time, Anne pausing in each doorway, not touching anything now, just looking long and hard, until we were in the great hall once more.

We sat at the table, leaning on our elbows and facing the fire, tranced by its drowsing; and all at once the fire was low and the room was chilled and we lifted our heads from our folded arms. We moved the bench closer to the hearth, threw our cloaks over our knees and leaned toward the fire.

"Ah Anne," I said, "I've news that must be told and I don't know how to tell it, especially here, in this room where we all gathered, where we all found such comfort."

Anne paused only an instant. Maybe she didn't pause at all.

"Bad news then," she said.

I nodded.

"Tell it then. And better to have it here, in this room, where we all gathered, and found comfort."

I told her all that Dinely had said.

I told her looking into the hearth.

She said nothing, did not stir or make a sound. When I looked at her again her eyes were closed.

"It was good of Dinely to come. And he was right." Her voice was flat. "They would have gone to excommunication, that was the ministers' plan. Mr. Cotton and Mr. Davenport were quite clear on that point. But it shan't happen. Now. I've seen to it. Taken measures . . . that had to be . . . it seemed the right thing, it must be, Mr. Cotton helped me and labored long over it . . . I hope you and all our friends, those remaining, can understand . . . Excommunication. Out of the community, out of communication: you know the Latin."

"You know I don't."

"*Communicare*, to make common. To make known to all, to make shared by all. My father used to say that all over the world at every moment bells were ringing and people were gathering as one to hear the same words that have been shared by all, made known to all, for thousands of years. If I were cast out of the church I would no longer be a part of that listening body, joined to all who have gone before and all who will be. That has been my strength. I believe it was my father's strength as well. I told you about him, Nell, what a man of conscience and conviction he was — once imprisoned, twice silenced for his opinions. But when he was given a parish that last time, I think he kept his own counsel and made peace with the church because he feared excommunication. I used to think it was for our sakes, Mother's and us children's, but later I realized it was for the sake of a larger family. I believed the one thing he feared, could not bear, was excommunication."

"And how is it with you? Is it any comfort that this is not your father's church, that it is a rebel church, a different one?"

"Even less comfort, far less. It was for this church that I left my father's tradition. It was for this church that I left the traditions of my childhood, it was for this that I left Alford, Lincolnshire, England — for this church. To make it all we hoped, to raise it up strong and hearty and whole; like parents with a child, we have cradled it and sacrificed for it, and yet at the same time we are all children of this church, in the end it is standing over us all. To tear this family bond from me would be more than I could bear, Nell. I cannot let that happen, no, cannot."

She leaned toward the fire, tears in her eyes.

"Ever since I was a child, churches have been my home. I

played in the empty naves, hid in the transepts, saw myself reflected in their windows, bathed my face in the fonts. I slept in them; waked in them. This Puritan church has become my new home, after all the others were left behind. The building has changed, the surface and form have changed, but the core of it is changeless and the core of it is the core of me. To be cast out of the colony, the visible community, that is hard. But I can bear it — just. To be cast out of that invisible community, the spiritual one — that is to be cast out of my own self . . . I must not, cannot let them do this."

"Did I do right in telling you?"

"Ah Nell, yes, I needed that warning."

"I cannot bear to see you go through another trial," I burst out. "Dear God, it's too much strain, you're ill and have been."

"I hope I'm not too weary to be clever."

"Little strength you'll have for any cleverness," I said, "if you don't get some proper rest now."

I fetched a quilt and she let me tuck her up on the bench with the high back near the hearth, and I sat with her until it was time. The room filled with changing lights and colors as the dawn broke and the sun rose, and shadows shifted across the walls and down the floor where all the people had come together for Anne's meetings, where all this had begun.

Anne, lying still and carefully arranged on the narrow bench, looked like a stone effigy of a queen on a church tomb, one that has been worn and rubbed by time and curious hands, cracks coming into the cast of the reposing face.

*O*nce again, and for the last time, we prepared to assemble at the meeting house. The week was up. We walked into this final moment of the ordeal through the most beautiful spring day I can ever remember in Boston.

Everywhere you looked, over meadows and front lots and the newer lanes, was a haze of tender green, like a green net spread out to dry in the sun. The fence posts sparkled from a wet night and the spider webs were dewy and delicate weavings, small odd flowers, purple and white were edging the lanes, and on the mild air you could see spring seed, faint flecks of it, flying.

The beauty of it. The cruelty of it.

They should have brought her in through rain.

They brought her in and they walked her down the aisle and they handed her a piece of paper to read. She read it so softly that the elders were constantly interrupting her, and none of us had any idea what it was about. No one could hear her. She was made to start again, she swayed, was given a stool and seated. And still when she read it again no one could hear her. At last John Cotton came forward and read it himself.

It was a recantation.

Not of the meetings. Nor anything said in them. Nothing of the controversy that had led to her imprisonment. But she had recanted all she had said to the ministers, as erroneous beliefs, during her imprisonment. That then, was her price, for not being excommunicated.

At the clergy's request, John Cotton rose to deliver a second admonition. He walked to the side of the meeting house where the women sit and addressed us.

"I remember the goodness she showed when she came here, in helping to reveal to others the false bottom they stood upon in trusting to legal works alone. But she has fallen into gross and fundamental errors. She has twisted our teachings."

Anne turned to him, clearly stunned, as if she had been slapped.

"She has lost the honor of her former service, and done more wrong to Christ and his church than she ever did good. She has laid heinous sins to her conscience. Women of Boston: although you have received some good from Mistress Hutchinson, all kindness received from her had poison mixed with it. All teaching received from her had poison mixed with it. You must make haste, I charge you, to vomit it up again."

"Mr. Cotton." Her voice shook. "I remind you that I only recanted what I said in prison this winter, not the meetings or anything taught at them. You assured me this would suffice, that this would be the end of it."

"Strike that from the record," Wilson shouted.

Anne continued to stare at Cotton's back, her expression slowly shifting from disbelief to pain, and comprehension.

Cotton went on, "I have long feared the height of your spirit and being puffed up in your own parts. I charge you to remember the great hurt you have brought upon Jesus Christ, the evil you have done to many a poor soul. Be jealous of your own spirit and take heed how you leaven the hearts of young women with such dangerous principles. We must now labor to recover them from the snares which you have drawn them into. May the Lord carry home to your soul all that I have spoken in his name!"

"My soul!" Anne spoke out clearly. "How can you pass judgment on my soul when you have betrayed your own?"

"Strike that," Wilson shouted again. "Mistress Hutchinson. You said you did not hold these errors before your imprisonment. Mr. Shepard says the contrary. What say you now?"

"If Mr. Shepard conceives that I had any of these things in my mind," Anne said, "then he is deceived."

Mr. Shepard sprang forward. "If this day Mrs. Hutchinson should take shame and confusion to her for her gross and damnable errors and instead casts shame upon others and says they are mistaken, I fear it does not stand with true repentance."

John Cotton, looking worried, stood beside her. "There are two things to be cleared. What do you believe now? What did you believe then?" He looked at her anxiously.

She did not move for an instant more when she lifted her head, took a breath, and rose, long fingers pressed together. She looked, not at the ministers, but straight back at the doors to the meeting house when she answered, her voice clear as glass.

"I believe what I have always believed. My judgment is not altered." She crossed the floor and took the recantation from Cotton's hands.

I sat there dazed. Now she would surely be excommunicated.

Dudley rose. "It matters not what Mistress Hutchinson does now. As for that recantation," he turned his gaze to Cotton, "whether she had any help with it I wonder, but will not now inquire into. But certainly her repentance was never on her countenance."

All the ministers' restraints seemed to break at once.

"The root of all your errors," Pastor Wilson spat, "is the

slighting of God's faithful ministers and condemning and crying them down as unworthies."

"I believe she has vile thoughts of us," said Hugh Peter, "and thinks us to be nothing but a company of Jews."

"This day we not only deal with a woman that never had any true grace in her heart, this day she has showed herself to be a false prophet," Shepard was shouting. "She has not only lied — she has maintained a lie in the sight of God."

Wilson turned to the ministers, "Consider how long we can suffer her to go on still in seducing to seduce, in deceiving to deceive, in lying to lie."

"The matter is now translated." Cotton spoke. "She has been dealt with in points of doctrine. Now she is dealt with in point of practice. And so it belongs to the pastor's office to instruct and correct in righteousness. I think we are bound upon this ground to remove her from us by excommunication, seeing she does prevaricate in her words."

Anne turned to Cotton and held his gaze.

"John Cotton. My teacher, my friend," she said, her voice level now. "John Cotton. How you have deceived me. You have become one of the archbishop's men. Look upon yourself. You have become one of that same tribe that persecuted you in England and chased you to your ship. You are running still."

"Strike it!" Wilson, red-faced, pounded the table for order. "We shall proceed to excommunication."

"How may the church proceed to excommunication when the Scripture says we must have mercy?" That was Mary Dyer's voice, coming cool and quiet beside me.

"Silence, woman!" Hugh Peter was on his feet. Pointing at Anne, "Get her out."

Mr. Leverett reminded them that the Scripture called for a second admonition before proceeding to excommunication. Dudley brushed this aside: "I would answer this to Mr. Leverett . . . Mistress Hutchinson hath been dealt with and admonished not once, or twice nor thrice, but many times by private brethren, the elders, by her own church."

Tom Savage was already speaking from his seat, urging Anne to say she had been distracted and now would throw herself on the court's mercy. But through those last moments, Anne sat looking out over our heads, as though she didn't hear him or the ministers.

At last she stood.

"Gentlemen," she addressed the ministers. "I have listened, amazed, at your words. I have been wondering, can this be the church that led me to leave the church of my father, the church of my village, my country itself? The body of the church is made of its members. The guiding members of this church are you, gentlemen, and I see now that I was in error — about you. There is a passage from Isaiah which was of great consolation to me before I came here. It promises that thine eyes shall see thy teachers. I see I misunderstood it. I thought you were my teachers. By your words, by your actions, by your very expressions you have shown me: that you are but men, and that the only teacher I must truly look to is God Almighty, the only words I must heed are His. *Thine ears shall hear a word behind thee saying this is the way.* You have power over my body but not over my soul. You are the body of this church but not its heart. The heart of the church is within us all and you have no power to cut me off from it. Proceed with your excommunication then . . . read your curse . . . It is made of men's words, not God's, and I fear it not."

She stood serenely as the meeting house went into uproar.

Wilson banged with both palms on the table for what seemed a long time before there was order again.

Wilson addressed the congregation. "The church consenting to it we will proceed to excommunication." He paused and motioned Anne to stand, as he rose and went to the pulpit.

Over her head he opened his book. She stood, but faced not him, nor any minister, but faced us.

"Forasmuch as you, Mistress Hutchinson, have highly transgressed and offended and troubled the church with your errors and have drawn away many a poor soul, and have upheld your revelations and forasmuch as you have made a lie . . ."

He paused and drew breath.

Her beautiful eyes were on us all, level and serene.

"I do cast you out and deliver you up to Satan and account you this time forth to be a heathen and a publican. I command you in the name of Christ Jesus and of this church to withdraw yourself as a leper out of this congregation."

I turned and rose and opened the door, holding it for her, so she could see . . . She stepped into the aisle.

Winthrop said, "May the Lord sanctify this unto you."

Anne paused at the head of the aisle, tilting her head to one side, but not turning round; she knew whose voice spoke.

Her voice, when she spoke, was clear; I could hear each word from my place in the doorway.

"The Lord does not judge as man judges," she said. "Better to be cast out of the Church than to deny God."

She walked slowly up the aisle. No one moved as she passed.

Halfway, Mary Dyer stood and stepped into the aisle. She linked her arm with Anne's, and they walked the rest of the way together.

Anne reached the open doors and took my hand and, without stopping, the three of us stepped over the sill. Our hems skimmed the flat stone step as we walked out into daylight, daylight so strong and keen we had to shade our eyes.

# EPILOGUE

*I* am just going.

It is not so hard to leave here as I had thought. Not now.

Easier to depart in anger than grief.

Yesterday the Reverend John Cotton, from the pulpit of Boston Church and before the entire town assembled for Divine Worship, recounted an act of Providence: a mother was brought to bed early with a monstrous birth, a babe that was not a babe, rather a gross mass of globular matter confusedly knit together, the whole of which Mr. Cotton described in such precise and bloody detail, the men in the congregation were paler than the women.

These details were gleaned from a doctor who had attended the birth, examined its issue, and made of it a written account — the examination and accounting both expressly requested by our own governor, John Winthrop. It is being said that the decision to read the account from the pulpit was John Cotton's.

The birth, he said, is a lesson; a Providential sign.

The sign manifests the evil of the woman, mother of a monster.

The name of the woman, read aloud in meeting, was Anne's.

How it pains me to think of her laboring through this

---

birth in agony of body, and recovering afterward in torment of spirit. How it pricks me to think that had I departed Boston sooner I might have been with her then.

And how it scalds me, the pride of these pious men, these ministers, elders, magistrates; this governor — these, our leaders in this divine experiment, these the elect, these the sanctified. If they be sanctified, then who be damned?

Nay, it will not be so hard, leaving here now.

I am amazed that my sleep is still able to hold dreams.

Every day this week I have laid away sheets and shifts and spoons and every night I have dreamed not of sheets or shifts or spoons, but of English fields.

When I was a child I went gleaning every year, following the reapers with my grandmother and the old folk who gleaned with the young, and by harvest tide's end I would have perhaps eight bushels of wheat.

Of this I dreamed last night and the nights before:

Going gleaning again in a yellow field, tireless as a child, gleaning again with grandma under a lavender sky. The reaper moves forward at an easy pace, I keep up without effort and the task is easy, my apron is full. The scythe glitters in the early evening light, the long light of late summer; it glows farther on, up ahead, higher still against the plumdark sky. So bright is the sickle it might be made of silver. It might even be the morning star.

Do I dream my death? But there is the joy of harvest tide, a ripeness to the dream; no fear, no sorrow there.

Perhaps I only dream of the journey before me.

There is a saying here in New England:

If you are too bad to stay in Massachusetts you go to Rhode Island and if you are too good to stay in Massachusetts you go to Connecticut.

It seems quite clear to me where that saying was composed.

It seems equally clear to me that the composer has good and bad muddled but never mind. Let it stand as it is.

---

Being too bad to stay in Massachusetts is good enough to suit me.

Proud I am to be following Anne's path.

I go to Rhode Island.

# ℋISTORICAL ᴀFTERWORD

*O*n March 28, 1638, Anne Hutchinson and her children joined William Hutchinson on land he had bought from the Narragansett Indians in what is now called Portsmouth, Rhode Island. He was one of the main organizers of the new community, whose civil compact was signed by nineteen Bostonians. Among them were William Coddington, who became the new governor, the Aspinwalls, the Balstons, the Coggeshalls, and the Dyers. Within a year Thomas and Faith Hutchinson Savage returned to Boston. William Hutchinson, who replaced William Coddington as governor for a year, died in Portsmouth in 1642 at the age of fifty-six. Anne Hutchinson moved with her younger children to land within Dutch jurisdictions, first to Long Island, and then to Pelham Bay in what is now Eastchester, New York, where she built a house, near other English settlers. Sometime during her fifty-second year, in late August of 1643, she and five of her youngest children — Francis, Anne, Mary, Katherine, William, and son-in-law William Collins — were massacred by Indians. Their bodies were placed in the new house with the livestock and the house was burned to the ground. One daughter, Susanna, was kidnapped by the Indians with whom she lived for at least two years before she was returned to the English. In Massachusetts Bay the news of the massacre was interpreted as another sign of Anne Hutchinson's sinfulness. A promontory on Pelham Bay is called Anne's Hoeck, but sources conflict over the origins of this title and the exact site of the Hutchinson house.

Ned Hutchinson eventually returned to Boston. Bridget Hutchinson married Thomas Sanford and continued in Rhode Island. After the death of Faith Hutchinson Savage, her husband Thomas Savage married the daughter of the Reverend Zachariah Symmes of Charlestown, Anne Hutchinson's first antagonist among the Massachusetts clergy. Among the many Hutchinson descendants was Thomas Hutchinson, the Tory governor of Massachusetts who was ousted during the American Revolution.

John Winthrop was re-elected as governor of Massachusetts in 1639 for another year's term. During the 1640's he functioned as magistrate, deputy governor, and governor again. He died at the age of sixty-one in 1649.

John Cotton became progressively more conservative after 1637 and gained renown throughout New England as a minister and author of works on congregational worship. With John Wilson he shared the pulpit of Boston Church until his death at age sixty-eight in 1652. He was the grandfather of the famous minister Cotton Mather.

John Wilson remained an advocate of orthodoxy and continued as pastor of Boston Church until his death in 1667. He was seventy-six.

William Dinely, the barber-surgeon, died during the winter of 1639 in a blizzard while on his way to extract a tooth.

Jane Hawkins, under suspicion of witchcraft, moved with her husband Richard to Braintree. In 1641 she was ordered to depart Massachusetts immediately by the General Court, and she moved to Portsmouth, Rhode Island.

Mary Dyer moved with her husband Will and her children to Rhode Island, having been banished and excommunicated in 1638, after the Hutchinsons' departure. The Dyers eventually settled in Newport. Mary Dyer delivered a eulogy to

Anne Hutchinson in Providence when news of the massacre reached Rhode Island. In 1652 she and her husband accompanied Roger Williams to England. When she returned to Massachusetts she had joined the Society of Friends. She became a minister of that faith and challenged Massachusetts' ban of Quakers, on pain of death, three times. The third time, in June of 1660, she was condemned and hanged on Boston Common.

The Hutchinson family's Boston house remained in the family until 1707, when it was bought by an apothecary, Thomas Creese. In 1715 Creese built a new house on the lot. In 1754 descendants of the Hutchinson family were again in possession of the property. The site, on the corner of what are now Washington and School Streets, was occupied until recently by the Old Corner Book Store and is now owned by the *Boston Globe.*

Today, in front of the State House of Massachusetts overlooking the Boston Common, stands a statue of Anne Hutchinson, honoring her contribution to the struggle for religious freedom in the New World.